At Issue

Should Social Networking Web Sites Be Banned?

Other Books in the At Issue Series:

At Issue

Should Social Networking Web Sites Be Banned?

Roman Espejo, Book Editor

GREENHAVEN PRESS

A part of Gale, Cengage Learning

GALE
CENGAGE Learning

Detroit • New York • San Francisco • New Haven, Conn • Waterville, Maine • London

Christine Nasso, *Publisher*
Elizabeth Des Chenes, *Managing Editor*

For more information, contact:
Greenhaven Press
27500 Drake Rd.
Farmington Hills, MI 48331-3535
Or you can visit our Internet site at gale.cengage.com

For product information and technology assistance, contact us at

Gale Customer Support, 1-800-877-4253
For permission to use material from this text or product, submit all requests online at
www.cengage.com/permissions

Further permissions questions can be emailed to permissionrequest@cengage.com

Articles in Greenhaven Press anthologies are often edited for length to meet page requirements. In addition, original titles of these works are changed to clearly present the main thesis and to explicitly indicate the author's opinion. Every effort is made to ensure that Greenhaven Press accurately reflects the original intent of the authors. Every effort has been made to trace the owners of copyrighted material.

LIBRARY OF CONGRESS CATALOGING-IN-PUBLICATION DATA

Should social networking web sites be banned? / Roman Espejo, book editor.
    p. cm. -- (At issue)
Includes bibliographical references and index.
ISBN-13: 978-0-7377-4058-5 (hardcover)
ISBN-13: 978-0-7377-4059-2 (pbk.)
1. Internet and teenagers. 2. Online social networks. 3. MySpace.com. 4. Internet--Social aspects. I. Espejo, Roman, 1977-
HQ799.2.I5S56 2008
302.23'1--dc22
                                                              2007048658

Printed in the United States of America
1 2 3 4 5 6 7 12 11 10 09 08

Contents

Introduction

In July 2007 social networking service MySpace identified and removed twenty-nine thousand known sex offenders' profiles from its Web site. This figure, however, only includes members who used their real names to register on MySpace and is more than quadruple the number MySpace had estimated earlier. It is presumed that many other sex offenders currently use MySpace, Friendster, Facebook, and other social networking Web sites with false identities or are not yet known by law enforcement. Also, by that time, about one hundred cases of adults using MySpace to commit crimes were publicly reported.

The presence of sexual offenders on social networking services like MySpace that are popular among teenagers spurred a movement to restrict minors' access to such Web sites. In May 2006 former Pennsylvania representative Michael G. Fitzpatrick introduced the Deleting Online Predators Act of 2006 (DOPA) to the House of Representatives, proposing to ban youths age seventeen and younger from accessing MySpace and similar Web sites at federally funded schools, libraries, and other institutions. The restriction would be lifted in specific cases if used "by an adult or by minors with adult supervision to enable access for educational purposes." Under this bill, a Web site could be defined as a social networking service if it:

is offered by a commercial entity;

permits registered users to create an online profile that includes detailed personal information;

permits registered users to create an online journal and share such a journal with other users;

elicits highly personalized information from users; and

enables communication among users.

That June, the House voted in favor of DOPA with a vote of 410–15. It was then turned over to the Senate, which did not vote on the bill. In January 2007 DOPA was reintroduced as part of the Protecting Children in the 21st Century Act, which was referred to the Commerce, Science, and Transportation Committee. A month later, it was reintroduced again as the Deleting Online Predators Act of 2007 and passed on to the House Committee on Energy and Commerce. As of early 2008, the bill has not been enacted.

Especially because a federal law such as DOPA does not currently exist, some contend that MySpace should implement age verification. The company currently allows members age fourteen and older to join, but automatically sets fourteen- and fifteen-year-olds' profiles to "private," restricting access to members on their "friends" list and members who are seventeen and younger. Because members' ages on MySpace can be falsified, North Carolina attorney general Roy Cooper strongly recommends that MySpace requires its teenage users to verify their age. Cooper believes that age verification should apply to social networking services as it does to alcohol and tobacco use, gambling, and motion pictures. In addition, he supports a North Carolina bill recently passed by the North Carolina Senate that would require minors to obtain permission from parents or legal guardians to become members of MySpace. Connecticut attorney general Richard Blumenthal proposes that MySpace should cross-check its members' ages using government databases. Blumenthal introduced a bill that would penalize social networking services five thousand dollars for each instance of incorrect age verification. Advocates insist that these measures would effectively prevent minors from lying about their ages and using MySpace in secret and simultaneously deter sexual predators from prowling such Web sites for potential victims. Social networking expert Dave Gormley even suggests that increased privacy could enhance users' social networking experience.

Detractors of age verification for MySpace and other social networks argue that it would not be effective and could be surreptitiously bypassed. Rick Lane, senior vice president of government affairs for News Corporation (which owns MySpace) states, "My son knows all my information, so there's nothing stopping him from signing on as me and giving himself permission to be on there." Lane alleges that "verification is a political solution, not a safety one." Also, others maintain that adequate age verification technologies simply do not exist, especially for free online services like MySpace, and would create a false sense of online security. Moreover, Adam Thierer, senior fellow and director for the Center for Digital Media Freedom, argues that "age verification raises many sensitive issues related to the privacy of children and online freedom of speech and expression. We need to avoid a rushed solution that too easily compromises those values." Thierer advises that, from social networking Web sites and other Internet applications, "we have actually gained some important advantages in our effort to combat child predation. Many of the predators leave digital tracks for us to follow. Thus, to the extent that disturbing things are happening online or being facilitated by the Internet in any fashion, at least there is a digital record of those activities or crimes."

The debate of age verification is one of the numerous issues involved with the potential ban on MySpace and other social networking services in public schools, libraries, and other institutions where minors can surf the Internet. In *At Issue: Should Social Networking Web Sites Be Banned?*, authors from different fields of expertise debate whether or not prohibiting access to social networks would enhance the safety of teenagers on the Internet.

1

MySpace and Other Social Networking Web Sites Should Be Banned

Michael G. Fitzpatrick

Michael G. Fitzpatrick is a politician and was a member of the U.S. House of Representatives, representing Pennsylvania's Eighth Congressional District from 2005 to 2007. In May 2006, he introduced the Deleting Online Predators Act of 2006 (DOPA).

The massive popularity of social networking Web sites like My-Space, Friendster, and Facebook, as well as chat rooms, undoubtedly brings people together. They come, however, with numerous risks, increasing minors' exposure to child predators, sexual solicitation, pornography, and bullying. Without parental supervision, children and teenagers are vulnerable to these dangers. Therefore, they should not be allowed to access these Web sites at schools or libraries. If enacted, the Deleting Online Predators Act would prohibit schools, libraries, and other institutions receiving federal funding from allowing minors to access social networking and similar Web sites. Though there is no single solution to ending the sexual exploitation of children, the enactment of this bill would further the protection and well-being of minors on the Internet.

Mr. Chairman,

Thank you for inviting me to participate in today's hearing and for allowing me to give testimony on what I feel is a

Michael G. Fitzpatrick, "Sexual Exploitation of Children on the Internet: How the State of New Jersey Is Combating Child Predators on the Internet," Before the Committee on Energy and Commerce Subcommittee on Oversight and Investigations, United States House of Representatives, June 10, 2006.

new and emerging problem confronting our nation's children and their safety while using the Internet. I am speaking of the rapid increase in popularity of Internet social networking sites and their use by child predators to hunt and harass our children at home, in schools and in our libraries.

As the father of six children, I know very well the challenges technology poses to our families. In a world that moves at a dizzying pace, being a father gets harder all the time. Monitoring our children's use of emerging technologies is a huge task and the Internet remains the focus of many parents' concerns.

A Worrying Development

The technological breakthrough of the World Wide Web has been enormously beneficial to society. The Internet has brought communities across the globe closer together through instant communication. It has enabled an unfiltered free-flow of thought, ideas and opinion. The Internet has opened a window to the world right at our fingertips. However, this window opens both ways. The freedom to connect to the world anywhere at anytime brings with it the threat of unscrupulous predators and criminals who mask their activities with the anonymity the Internet provides to its users. And among its many applications, one of the most worrying developments of late has been the growth in what are known as "social networking sites."

Social networking sites like MySpace, Friendster, and Facebook have literally exploded in popularity in just a few short years. MySpace alone has almost 90 million users and ranks as the sixth most popular English language website and the eighth most popular site in the world.

Anyone can use these sites—companies and colleges, teachers and students, young and old all make use of networking sites to connect with people electronically to share pictures, information, course work, and common interests. These sites have torn down the geographical divide that once prevented long distance social relationships from forming, allowing instant communication and connections to take place and a virtual second life to take hold for its users.

For adults, these sites are fairly benign. For children, they open the door to many dangers including online bullying and exposure to child predators that have turned the Internet into their own virtual hunting ground. I became personally aware of the danger the Internet can pose after my 16-year-old daughter began using the social networking site MySpace.com. I quickly realized that while my daughter thought she was only chatting with her friends, other people, some with criminal intent, could be looking in.

No Enforcement

Although age limits exist on many of these sites, there is almost no enforcement of these rules. Frequently, children under the age of 16—the cut off age for a profile on MySpace [fourteen as of April 2007]—simply lie about their age and fake being 16, 18 or even older. Predators also use this anonymity to their advantage by profiling themselves as teenagers to more easily identify and navigate the profiles of their prey.

The dangers our children are exposed to by these sites is clear and compelling. According to a study conducted by the National Center for Missing and Exploited Children (NCMEC), in 1998 there were 3,267 tips reporting child pornography. Since then, the number has risen by over 3,000 percent to an astounding 106,119 tips in 2004. The Department of Justice recognizes child pornography as a precursor for pedophiles and is often linked to online predators. According to Attorney General [Alberto] Gonzales, one in five children has been approached sexually on the Internet. One in five. Worse still, a survey conducted by the Crimes Against Children Research Center found that less than one in four children told their parents about the sexual solicitation they received. My-

Space, which is self regulated, has removed an estimated 200,000 objectionable profiles since it began operating in 2003. And while it is difficult to predict the exact number of total predators on the Internet at any one time, the Federal Bureau of Investigation (FBI) estimates that there are more than 2,400 active child sexual exploitation investigations under way at any given time.

This problem is finally gaining the public's attention. Look closely at local and national news stories and you will undoubtedly see a story of a crime linked to social networking sites. Recently, national news reports have focused on the case of Katherine R. Lester, a 16-year-old Michigan honors student who fled to Israel with hopes of meeting a 25-year-old man she met on MySpace. Two months ago, in my own congressional district, a 25-year-old man, Shawn Little, was arrested for posing as a teenager online to solicit a 14-year-old boy. Little's communications with the child resulted in a sexual encounter. And NBC's *Dateline* program has brought the threat of online predators to the televisions of millions of Americans through their acclaimed, but disturbing, "To Catch a Predator" series. While these high-profile cases make a splash on the headlines, how many other, less publicized cases of child exploitation go unnoticed?

While these [child predator] stories have pressured many social networking sites to take action to improve their safety protocol, like MySpace has recently done, these changes fall short of real reform.

The Deleting Online Predators Act

While these stories have pressured many social networking sites to take action to improve their safety protocols, like MySpace has recently done, these changes fall short of real reform. That is why I introduced the Deleting Online Predators Act.

Parents have the ability to screen their children's Internet access at home. But this protection ends when their child leaves for school or the library. My legislation would require schools and libraries to monitor the internet activities of minors and implement technology to protect children from accessing:

1. Commercial networking sites like MySpace.com and chat rooms which allow children to be preyed upon by individuals seeking to do harm to our children; and

2. Visual depictions that are obscene or child pornography.

Preventing access to social networking sites in these situations is not designed to underestimate the importance of parental supervision. Internet safety begins at home and that is why my legislation would require the Federal Trade Commission [FTC] to design and publish a unique website to serve as a clearinghouse and resource for parents, teachers and children for information on the dangers of surfing the Internet. The website would include detailed information about commercial networking sites. The FTC would also be responsible for issuing consumer alerts to parents, teachers, school officials and others regarding the potential dangers of internet child predators and their ability to contact children through MySpace.com and other social networking sites.

Predators will look for any way to talk to children online whether through sites like MySpace, instant messaging, or even online games.

In addition, my Bill would require the Federal Communications Commission to establish an advisory board to review and report commercial social networking sites like MySpace .com and chat rooms that have been shown to allow sexual predators easy access to personal information of, and contact with, children.

Make no mistake; child predation on the Internet is a growing problem. Predators will look for any way to talk to children online whether through sites like MySpace, instant messaging, or even online games. The best defense against these people is to educate parents and children of the dangers that come along with the Internet and by limiting access to certain sites during the school day.

No "Silver Bullet" Solution

This is not all. Congress and state legislatures must also act to dedicate funds to law enforcement programs designed to combat child predators. Last month, I actively fought for and Congress passed legislation to increase funding to the FBI's Internet Crimes Against Children Task Forces and the Innocent Images National Initiative, which serves as the hub for all of the FBI's child predator initiatives. Supporting these programs will send a clear signal to child predators and pedophiles that the hunters have become the hunted and law enforcement will not relent until these criminals are apprehended.

There is no "silver bullet" solution to the problem of online predators. It will take the combined effort of parents, children, law enforcement and the legislature to take action against these crimes. Thank you, Mr. Chairman, for inviting me to address this committee and remark on my efforts to address this important issue.

2

MySpace and Other Social Networking Web Sites Should Not Be Banned

Part I: Bart Stupak, Part II: American Library Association

Part I: Since 1993, Bart Stupak has been a Democratic member of the U.S. House of Representatives, representing Michigan's First Congressional District. Part II: Founded in 1876, the American Library Association (ALA) is the oldest association of libraries in the world. It is also the largest association of its kind, with over sixty-four thousand members.

Part I: The Deleting Online Predators Act of 2006 (DOPA), which would ban minors from accessing MySpace and other social networks in schools, libraries, and other federally funded institutions, does not address the problem of online child exploitation. Children and teenagers are most vulnerable online in their own homes without adult supervision. If enacted, DOPA will actually compel minors to visit social networking Web sites in places without any supervision whatsoever, leaving them even more vulnerable.

Part II: The enactment of DOPA and a ban on social networking Web sites in schools and libraries should be opposed for several reasons. Because of the act's broad language, many useful Web sites and Internet-based applications would be blocked to the detriment of education. Poor students would also be unfairly affected by DOPA, as they are not likely to have Internet access at home. Moreover, such a ban would be redundant because of

Bart Stupak, American Library Association, "Deleting Online Predators Act of 2006, the United States House of Representatives," *Congressional Record*, Section 41, July 26, 2006.

preexisting local laws in many areas. Finally, prohibiting access instead of educating students on how to use the Internet does not promote their safety.

M r. Speaker, I take a back seat to no one when it comes to my dedication to tracking down, prosecuting and locking up child predators. I have helped lead the child predator investigation in the House [of Representatives], and I have participated in six hearings on this issue.

Many schools and libraries already block Web sites such as MySpace. This legislation is largely redundant and raises many constitutional concerns.

Unfortunately, child predators are not the target of today's bill [the Deleting Online Predators Act of 2006 (DOPA)]. This bill will not delete online predators. Rather, it will delete legitimate Web content from schools and libraries. Schools and libraries that serve students are the target of this legislation.

The bill is an attempt to protect children in schools and libraries from online predators. It is important to note that during the six oversight hearings we had, hearing from 38 witnesses on the issue, there was not one mention of online child exploitation being a problem at schools or libraries. Perhaps this is because there is already a law on the books that requires schools and libraries who receive e-rate funding [federal government funding to help schools and libraries pay for Internet services] to monitor children's Internet use and to employ technology blocking children or preventing children from viewing obscene and harmful content.

The National School Boards Association [NSBA] opposes this bill saying, "NSBA is concerned that the bill would not substantially improve safety of students, and would place an added and unnecessary burden on schools. Furthermore, the legislation does not address the real issue of educating children about the dangers of the Internet and how to use it responsibly and wisely."

The American Library Association also opposes this bill, saying the bill "denies access to constitutionally protected speech."

The Real Threat to Our Children

This bill will not tackle the real threat to our children. Our committee learned from teens, experts and law enforcement that the real threat lies in children using these sites in their rooms without adult supervision.

This legislation will actually drive children to go to unsupervised places, unsupervised sites to go online, where they will become more vulnerable to child predators.

Finally, and importantly, legislation before us today does nothing to hold Internet service providers [ISPs] accountable. We learned from our hearings that ISPs vary widely in what they do to empower children and parents, how they report online predators to authorities, and actively seek and block illegal content from their networks.

The bottom line is that Members can vote for this bill, but we should not give parents the false hope that this bill will keep their children safe. This bill will increase the risk to children as we drive children away from supervised sites to unsupervised sites.

Finally, Mr. Speaker, I am profoundly disappointed that this issue that should not be a partisan issue is becoming one.

Part II

I will enter into the *record* at this point the letter of opposition from the American Library Association.

American Library Association,

Washington, DC, July 26, 2006.

Dear Representative: On behalf of the American Library Association (ALA), I write to indicate our continued opposition to H.R. 5319, the Deleting Online Predators Act (DOPA). We understand this bill may come to the House floor this afternoon and ask that you oppose this bill as it presently reads.

No profession or community is more concerned about the safety of children than our Nation's librarians. Librarians in public libraries and school library media centers work continuously to assure that children have appropriate and safe access to the materials and information services they need so that each young person can become literate and educated with the skills and knowledge to succeed in the digital and online world.

Young people must be prepared to thrive in a work atmosphere where meetings take place online, where online networks are essential communication tools.

ALA had hoped following the July 11th hearing on H.R. 5319 before the Commerce Committee's Subcommittee on Telecommunications and the Internet, that an amended version would seek to resolve some of the problems we expressed in ALA's testimony. Unfortunately, the revised language we received only last night does not make the necessary changes that we believe would better serve the public interest and contribute to true online safety for young people. We urge opposition to H.R. 5319 for several reasons:

1. The terminology used in DOPA is still overly broad and unclear. As written, this legislation would block access to many valuable websites that utilize this type of communication, websites whose benefits outweigh their detriments.

2. DOPA still ignores the value of Interactive Web applications. New Internet-based applications for collaboration, business and learning are becoming increasingly important, and young people must be prepared to thrive in a work atmosphere where meetings take place online, where online networks are essential communication tools.

3. Education, not laws blocking access, is the key to safe use of the Internet. Libraries and schools are where kids learn essential information literacy skills that go far beyond computer instruction and web searching. Indeed, DOPA would block usage of these sites in the very environments where librarians and teachers can instruct students about how to use all kinds of applications safely and effectively and where kids can learn how to report and avoid unsafe sites.

4. Local decision-making—not federal law—is the way to solve the problems addressed by DOPA. Such decisions are already being made locally, in part due to the requirements of the Children's Online Protection Act (CIPA) for E-rate recipients. This additional requirement is not necessary.

5. DOPA would restrict access to technology in the communities that need public access most. H.R. 5319 still, as presently drafted, would require libraries and schools receiving E-rate discounts through the Universal Service Program to block computer users from accessing Interactive Web applications of all kinds, thereby limiting opportunities for those who do not have Internet access at home. This unfairly denies the students and library users in schools and libraries in the poorest communities from accessing appropriate content and from learning how best to safely manage their own Internet access in consultation with librarians and teachers.

It should also be noted that key witnesses at the July 11th [2006] hearing testified that limiting access to social networking sites in E-rate schools and libraries will have little impact on the overall problem since young people access these collaborative sites from many locations and over a period of time. . . .

Thank you for your consideration.

Sincerely,

Director, Office of Government Relations

3

MySpace Should Be Used as a Teaching Tool and Not Be Banned

Christopher Harris

Christopher Harris is coordinator of the School Library System for Genesee Valley BOCES, the Boards of Cooperative Educational Services, in New York State.

The media depict social networking Web sites like MySpace as notoriously dangerous, brimming with sexual predators and stalkers. However, social networking is viewed as a threat because it largely belongs to the insular, chaotic world of teenagers, which many adults do not understand. Instead of shunning these Web sites, schools should use social networking to reach out to and teach students. For example, art and music teachers can encourage budding artists and musicians to share their work online. Also, the problems presented by social networks—bullying, violence, and hate speech—can be used as platforms for meaningful discussions in social studies classrooms. All in all, it is in young people's best interest that schools teach them to participate in online communities safely and sensibly.

I'm sure that the headlines and their dire warnings about cyberstalkers help sell papers and convince TV viewers to stay tuned to hear about the latest threat to their children, but this whole MySpace ban needs to stop.

Christopher Harris, "MySpace Can Be Our Space: Let's Turn the Infamous Networking Site into a Teachable Moment," *School Library Journal*, vol. 52, May 2006, p. 30. Copyright © 2006. Reproduced from *School Library Journal*, a Cahners/R.R. Bowker publication, by permission.

After all, the social networking Web site that is all the rage among teens, is, as Kevin Poulsen explained in a February 2006 *Wired* magazine article, "TheirSpace not OurSpace". Adults just don't get it. At first glance, as Poulsen writes, "a typical [MySpace] page is a near perfect reflection of the chaos and passion of youth: a music-filled space, rudely splattered with photos and covered in barely-legible prose." Add to that reports of sexual predators prowling the site, and no wonder there's been a crackdown on MySpace at schools across the country.

Recent Internet history, however, suggests this may not be the best approach. When music piracy became the big problem a few years ago, suing [the music file-sharing service] Napster out of existence sure put a stop to music downloading, didn't it?

A Teaching Tool

A more effective approach is to utilize MySpace as a teaching tool. These lessons can be embedded into a variety of classes and subjects.

Art. Perhaps the greatest concern about MySpace involves its role as a public gallery for posting pictures. Art teachers can take this opportunity to spark a dialogue on what is appropriate imagery for public and private display. (Though certainly the inclusion of pictures that portray illegal or sexually explicit acts isn't up for debate.) And there are some wonderful examples of photography on the Web site that showcase truly inspired work by young artists. Highlighting such positive examples and inviting student debate and discussion can encourage appropriate use of the site. Students also need to understand that pictures they think are OK may be scandalous to adults, including college admissions personnel or potential employers.

Social Studies. Many schools have taken issue with MySpace over online threats of violence and other hate speech.

Related discussions—appropriate for social studies class-rooms—could focus on the pertinent protections and limitations of the free speech clause of the First Amendment. According to legal precedent, threats of violence or harm are one of the few types of speech not protected by the Constitution.

In addition, a New York case established that students who engage in such speech, even if they do it outside of school, can be punished by the school if they "endanger the health or safety of pupils within the educational system or adversely affect the educative process" (*Coghlan v. Board of Education*, 262 AD2d 949 [4th Dept. 1999]). It will be interesting to see how recent cases involving MySpace, and similar Web sites, address this issue.

Music. And then there's the issue of copyright infringment. Many youngsters have adapted protected works, such as music and song lyrics, onto their personal MySpace pages. (Ironically enough, MySpace was founded, in part, to help musicians connect with their audience.) Here, music teachers could empower students by helping them become content creators, who share original material rather than simply duplicate the work of others.

In the end, schools need to face the music and tune in to MySpace.

Our Best Bet

In the end, schools need to face the music and tune in to MySpace. If districts simply block access to these sites and fail to address the issues surrounding online communities and digital personas, then it is unjust for schools to punish students for their online actions. As educators begin talking to students about these issues, however, I hope they will address the dangers, while also sharing the great potential of these sites.

MySpace and other social networking sites are among the fastest growing areas of the Internet. It is unreasonable to think that they'll simply go away. Our best bet is to become part of the conversation and help youngsters make good, safe decisions, as they join the online community.

4

MySpace and Other Social Networking Web Sites Are Dangerous for Children

Domenick Maglio

Domenick Maglio is the director of Wider Horizons, a college preparatory school for elementary and high school students. He also has worked as a clinical psychologist and is the author of Essential Parenting *and* Invasion Within. *Maglio lives in Hernando County, Florida.*

MySpace and other online social networks are viewed by young people as "cool" and sophisticated and beckon them to boost their popularity, page visits, and number of "friends" with provocative profiles. Consequently, such Web sites are dangerous places for children and adolescents. Inexperienced and naive, they share their biographical information, interests, location, and inviting photos for the world to see on these Web sites, not realizing that child predators are constantly prowling the Internet. Therefore, parents must teach their children the dangers of logging on to the fantasy worlds social networks create and to not use them in secret.

The days of thinking children are safe in their own rooms, in their secure gated communities, are gone. Children as young as eight years old are going into cyberspace to expand their universe. They travel without an understanding of the dangers to which they are exposed. This site [MySpace], like "Facebook" for college students, contains photos that verge on soft porn. The difference is younger children are flocking to "MySpace." Parents of young children are obliged to go online and browse the website www.myspace.com to judge for themselves.

You will not be alone. Although under many parents' radar screen, over 40 million mostly young people throughout the world use this site to become virtual friends with total strangers. Over 87% of youth in the twelve to seventeen age bracket are actively involved online. Ask your ten-year-old about MySpace and he will probably have some knowledge of it. The concept of being highlighted online is spreading like wildfire in the youth culture. It is seen as being sophisticated.

The real danger to our children is that there are many deviant people who can view the child's website by only clicking on their picture, name, address, or zip code.

Too Much Idle Time

In our fragmented existence, children have little responsibility in helping the family and too much idle time on their hands to create a fantasy existence. As the proverb states, "An idle mind is the devil's workshop". Our youth, with their abundance of unsupervised time, are writing up biographical sketches with often provocative photos exposing too much skin and too much information to attract new so-called "friends." The interests and photos are usually altered to present an image of what she wants to be rather than what she really is. There is no easier way to develop an identity than to instantly project one to an unknown audience. Most modern young people know more about the perverted world of Hollywood than they do about their own relatives. On MySpace anyone is given a stage to be a celebrity to an anonymous audience.

Children feel invincible. They may have been taught the dangers of being online, but they think any problems would never happen to them, only to someone else. The real danger to our children is that there are many deviant people who can view the child's website by only clicking on their picture, name, address or zip code, by this simple procedure your daughter or son becomes vulnerable to become the next potential victim of a predator.

Do not feel too complacent if your child is younger than fifteen years old. According to the guidelines of MySpace anyone under the age of fifteen would have a limited website viewed only by their friends who have their email. However, there is no check on any material entered on the site, including age, so younger children often make themselves appear older.

The Seductiveness of MySpace

MySpace is not a master plan to gain access to children. It is an enterprise for making a profit. The business purpose of MySpace is to make money through advertising. The more people driven to the site, the more a business can be charged for ads.

MySpace has found a surefire way to increase traffic to its site. It provides a vehicle for youngsters to become "popular" at least online and in their own minds. The seductiveness of MySpace for children is to develop a network of "friends." The more risqué the photo, the more hits you get. You are advertising yourself to get people to click on to contact you. The number of "friends" is listed on the person's website, so the more friends, the greater the bragging rights of being "cool."

Young people placing their photos and interests online is a frightening process for those of us with life experience. Children with a limited number of years on Earth have an equally limited knowledge of human nature. More and more stories are appearing with people who have met an evil person online and have come to a bad end. The unlimited access to millions of people will only add to the number of these tragedies.

There is no denying that cyberspace is a reality of modern times. There are no foolproof means of ensuring our children are not venturing into this precarious world except one: their word. We need to depend on our children pledging themselves to do what they say they do. They must tell the truth.

Instilling a moral code in your children by teaching them to be honest will prevent them from doing things behind your back. The cost of embarrassing one's parents becomes too great to distort their personal history to impress others.

Involved parents are the antidote to the world of ever-expanding temptation. Stronger parenting will stop "boys and girls going wild" into the dangerous world of online fantasy and into the arms of waiting predators.

5

Social Networking Plays an Important Role in Young People's Lives

Gary Stager

Gary Stager is senior editor for District Administration *magazine and an adjunct professor at Pepperdine University.*

Hysteria over MySpace is merely the latest example of adult concern about effects of new media. Social networking has value in the lives of today's teens and the electronic democracy it provides should be celebrated. Just as the unsettling, violent images and lyrics found in comic books, heavy metal, and rap music were blamed for teenage delinquency and antisocial behavior in the past, the social phenomenon MySpace is targeted by adults and the media as being an adulterated Web site where children and teens are bombarded by explicit content and hounded by sexual predators. And although the contents and chaos of many teenagers' profiles, like their bedrooms, will shock most adults, MySpace serves as a much needed place for teenagers to create their own space and hang out.

During seventh grade a friend and I created a publication as an alternative to the school newspaper. It was quite a challenge in the days before access to photocopiers, but entertaining our handful of readers made the effort worthwhile.

I remember the day when the faculty advisor of the official school newspaper followed me into the boy's room, threw my 50-pound body against the wall and threatened to kill me if we published another issue. The English faculty's Tony Soprano really schooled me in the subtleties of the First Amendment. Ah, life was so much simpler then.

Since man first scribbled on cave walls and peed in the snow, humans have been compelled to share their stories. Recent decades have seen great violence done to student expression through court-sanctioned censorship of student publications and other forms of adult supremacy. Issues of critical importance and interest to students are banned from student newspapers and classroom discussions. Political correctness and tolerance are used to masquerade for intolerant policies like "zero-tolerance" and increasingly mediocre curriculum. High school credit is awarded just to get kids to contribute to some school newspapers.

Back in the good old days of lavatory justice, children climbed trees, played ball in the street and joined the scouts so they could play with fire. Santa delivered chemistry sets complete with recipes for gunpowder and kids could get together without having "my people call your people." You could actually read all 30 pages of *Sarah Plain and Tall* without a textbook publisher excerpting it for you. Remember when you could read a book without being interrupted every paragraph to answer a comprehension question?

Same Problems, Modern Times

Parents and educators have done a lot more to wreck childhood than [inventor of the World Wide Web] Tim Berners-Lee (ask a kid to show you how to learn about him at Wikipedia). Schools endanger the very students they seek to protect when they bubble-wrap kids and the curriculum. School principals are banning classic plays like *Grease* and *The Crucible* while childish schlock like *Seussical* is now the most performed high school musical. John Taylor-Gatto argues that the mission of schools is now to extend childishness through graduation. Dependency and fear retard the learning process. It is difficult, if not impossible, for students to develop moral values and solve ethical dilemmas when school never allows them to make a decision or mistake.

Much of MySpace's content is inane, but we should avoid destroying the place 21st century kids built for themselves.

Every generation has had to wrestle with understanding new media. In 1954, the U.S. Senate held hearings to investigate how comic books harm children. Who can forget Tipper Gore vs. Frank Zappa [who testified as opponents at a senate hearing on porn rock] or the 1995 *Time* magazine cover depicting a computer-induced zombie child with CyberPorn in block letters? The educational technology community has a similar level of paranoia manifest in discussions over whether students should have their own floppy, be allowed to save on the hard drive, surf the Web, send an e-mail or use a USB key. It is impossible to discern the lines between genuine safety concerns and tyranny.

The latest episode of adults behaving badly involves the hysteria over the popular Web site, MySpace. MySpace is a social networking site where anyone can publish and maintain relationships with friends. Chances are that your only experience with MySpace has come through local TV news stories about how parents must rescue their teenagers from this deadly cyber-sewer before sports and weather. It's a fair bet that you are not one of MySpace's 66 million registered users [over 190 million as of July 2007]. There has probably never been a more aptly named product. They call it MySpace because it belongs to them, not you.

MySpace provides users with Web space where they may share their thoughts and creative output with classmates and friends around the world. What makes sites like MySpace different from other blogging sites is that you may ask interesting people to be your friend. Then you'll know when your friends are online, who their friends are and quickly develop affinity groups. You may organize communities around interests, geography or a host of other variables. You can chat via instant messages, insert music in your page and share all the photos and doodads that kids use to decorate their locker. (If school still trusts them with lockers.)

The recent student walkouts over the proposed immigration bill were organized on MySpace. The role such sites play in grassroots and electoral politics is inestimable.

In fact; more than one observer has compared MySpace pages to a teenager's bedroom walls. My 12th grade daughter's MySpace site is unbearable. Animated gifs, flashing graphics, dopey poses, horrific music, yellow text on hot pink backgrounds and other elements of Web design hell assault your senses until you run away or quit the browser. Much of MySpace's content is inane, but we should avoid destroying the place 21st century kids built for themselves.

Risks of MySpace Are Avoidable

Sure there are creeps using MySpace. That's why you need to teach children not to share personal information online or get in a car with strangers. MySpace never shows the real name of a member, just a pseudonym like a CB radio handle. When you add a person to your friends list, that person receives an e-mail asking for permission. If someone turns out to be unpleasant, you may ban him or her from contacting you with a click. Even critics of MySpace concede the company is incredibly responsive to concerns over online ickyness. A student may be at greater risk of being suspended by her school for something written at home on MySpace as there is of that teenager being physically harmed.

MySpace is changing how young people communicate, collaborate and spend their discretionary funds. Network TV programs are being launched on MySpace and countless bands have experienced enormous sales due to word-of-mouth and users sharing music with their friends. The recent student walkouts over the proposed immigration bill were organized on MySpace. The role such sites play in grassroots and electoral politics is inestimable.

Today my daughter's high school experienced a small fire. She learned of the fire from friends via MySpace nearly 11 hours before the local television news reported it. MySpace is a teenager's record store, newsstand, community center, fan club and 24/7 news network. As our government strives to spread democracy abroad, we would be well served by celebrating the electronic democracy afforded by sites like MySpace.

I just learned that my daughter has retaliated for me showing her MySpace site in conference presentations by posting an unflattering photo of me online. I wonder if I can get the local school district to punish her?

6

Sexual Predators Use MySpace and Other Networking Sites to Find Victims

John Carlin

John Carlin is a coanchor and managing editor at Newschannel 10, the NBC affiliate in Roanoke, Virginia.

Although children and teenagers have been warned to never reveal personal information online, showcasing such information, along with suggestive and revealing photos, is part of MySpace and other social networks' appeal. Unfortunately, sexual predators are drawn in droves to these Web sites for the same reasons. Not only does MySpace provide photos, biographical information, and the locations of potential victims, it has a search feature that allows predators to pursue the child or teenager of their choice. Therefore, it is no surprise that sexual exploitation cases related to MySpace and similar Web sites are on the rise. In response, parents must be vigilant in supervising their children's Internet habits and online profiles.

It wasn't so long ago we told our kids not to give away personal information on the internet. We told them don't give your address, your hobbies, or where you go to school. Don't release your phone number or your parents' names. The concern was that stalkers would be able to piece the information together and find young Johnny or Jane and molest/abduct them.

John Carlin, "My Space: Predator's Paradise," *WSLS.com*, February 8, 2006. Reproduced by permission. www.wsls.com/servlet/Satellite?pagename=WSLS/MGArticle/SLS_BasicArticle&;c=MGArticle&cid=1137834396486.

Yet somehow, a new website called MySpace has stormed the internet in the past year [2005] with nothing but personal information—and that's what *makes* it so popular.

Are you a swinger? Gay, Straight or Bi-sexual? Questions that go way beyond the basics we tell our kids not to give out in chat rooms. Yet there is an actual form that people with MySpace accounts fill out when they sign up. It gives away that information and a lot more.

"If you had asked somebody a year ago how they felt about MySpace and would it be where it's at today, nobody would have thought it would," says Bedford County [Virginia] Sheriff's deputy Lt. Mike Harmony who oversees the Department's *Blue Ridge Thunder* project designed to catch internet predators.

In addition to the information, account holders also post photos of themselves and their friends. Harmony and others contend that many of the pictures are suggestive in nature and that adds to the likelihood that a predator will come calling.

"We routinely see teenage girls clad only in swim suits or their undergarments," he said. "Creeps will copy those and send them all over the internet. Those can never be gotten back."

A common technique predators use is to pose as a fellow teen.

Harmony and deputy Rodney Thompson show me a computer file of predators they've arrested and successfully prosecuted. Each has some connection to the area. Either they lived here, had relations with a local girl or boy or traveled here thinking they might have the chance.

The people in the computer file used chat rooms, not MySpace—but the Blue Ridge Thunder Team expects that to change.

Carlin: "How does MySpace compare to everything else on the internet?"

Mike Harmony: "It's the up and coming trend."

More and More Time Policing MySpace

Harmony explains that his Blue Ridge Thunder team is spending more and more time policing MySpace. He says it poses some unique challenges—and opportunities for predators. We sit at his computer in a room where officers spend much of their time trying to catch stalkers in the act. He pulls up a MySpace account. "You're seeing an attractive young girl here, but the attractive girl you are seeing may be a 50-year-old guy," he said. A common technique predators use is to pose as a fellow teen. They then try to get the teen to meet them at the mall or somewhere else, where they might take advantage of them.

The men in the file are scary beyond a parent's imagination. If I had any doubts that people would actually go to those lengths to trick a teenager or pre-teen, the file erased them.

Some examples:

Raymond Cannup then of Bedford, screen name Dr. Evil. Caught by police on his way to meet what he thought was a young girl. He was carrying only duct tape, an ax handle and a fishing knife in his car.

Timothy May of Appomattox—had pornographic photos of minor girls he met online on his computer. Police say he had distributed them on the internet.

Joshua Deel of Bedford, screen name "gotmilki" and "xacidklownx."

Harmony describes some of Deel's offenses. "He met two different girls in Bedford County. Both of them minors. Had sex with both the girls after meeting them online." Harmony says Deel also took naked pictures of the girls and threatened to post them on the internet if they told about the encounters. Harmony says the girls didn't know he had posted the photos anyway.

There are dozens of cases—and the chat conversations leave no doubt as to a predator's intentions.

Another convict—35-year-old James Colbert—an army Sergeant arrested after the following chat with an officer posing as a 13-year-old girl.

> "Girl": You asked if I wanted to (bleep) you. . . . How would that happen?
>
> Colbert: Pick you up in my car. Carry u to my bedroom. . . . Slowly undress you and make love. Put a condom on and do it slow, because I know it will hurt. . . .
>
> Another chat. This time from Paul Glass of Hurt, Virginia.
>
> "Girl": I'm 13 how about u?
>
> Glass: I want someone I can make love to. . . . You too young for me unless you want an older man. . . .
>
> Then later . . .
>
> Glass: Call me. You will love the way I will make your (bleep) feel.
>
> "Girl": . . . yea right. When?
>
> Glass: Anytime you want. . . . You don't live far . . . and we can work this out.

Learning the Patterns

Rodney Thompson is often the officer posing as the young girl. He's learned the patterns.

"Predators who look for young girls are typically looking to get involved in relationships and they are looking for the word quote unquote, 'love.' . . . Over the course of time we find they might have 5–6 real victims over their lifetime or up until they get caught."

He says men seeking boys are even more aggressive.

"Typically I would say the typical male engaged in say a homosexual male with adult males as well as juvenile males you might run into say 20–40 different victims over a lifetime."

The predators in this story were all in chat rooms. But police tell me that MySpace and new look-alike sites will eventually make chat rooms passé.

Beyond the pictures and the abundance of information that predators crave is the MySpace search feature that allows predators to pick and choose their victims.

Beyond the pictures and the abundance of information that predators crave is the MySpace search feature that allows predators to pick and choose their victims. We searched for minor teenagers in Roanoke County and found:

Harmony: "771 minors met our search criteria within 5 miles of Roanoke."

What are the chances that one of them might accept an invitation to join this man in his hot tub? A standard pick-up line offered by Leonard Hudson, another man in the Blue Ridge Thunder file.

Or another man, James Reed, who bragged to the judge that he had had sex with 6 adult women, 5 men, 23 children and a dog.

There's no doubt that teens love the site and many are just talking to their friends.

But parents will need to keep watch. Because there's no doubt that internet predators like those in Harmony's file are watching too.

Again I want to emphasize that the convicted on-line predators we showed you in this story were all arrested prior to the popularity of MySpace. They are included in the story to demonstrate the danger to MySpace users who are not careful.

Five Things Parents Should Do

Here are five things parents should do to protect your kids from the dangers of MySpace.

1. Realize that many teens have two accounts, one they show you and a "racier" one they don't.
2. If they have a MySpace account, ask them not to fill out the answers to the survey.
3. Don't allow the posting of enticing photos. Remember once they are on the internet there is no way to get them back.
4. Don't allow your teen to accept any "friends" they don't know—even if they appear to be other teenagers.
5. Ask your teen or pre-teen to sit down and go over the site with you.

7

Social Networking Web Sites May Be Used to Distribute Child Pornography

InformationWeek

InformationWeek *is a weekly magazine on business and technology.*

Child pornography exists on social networks like Second Life, a multiplayer online virtual world where users create identities and role play. Depictions of virtual children being tortured and sexually exploited on such Web sites are a serious problem, as actual images of children have been allegedly used. Also, despite the concerted efforts of law enforcement, social networks have exacerbated the online distribution of child pornography. However, social networks are coming to terms with this issue, and Second Life enforces a zero-tolerance policy for pornographic content depicting children.

Illegal though it may be, child pornography and its virtual variants remain relatively common online. Responding to [online virtual world Second Life vice president Robin] Harper's blog entry, someone posting under the name ColeMarie Soleil claimed, "There is *tons* of child-to-adult sex going on in Second Life."

Not everyone sees that as a problem. Some Second Life [SL] residents who commented on Harper's blog post criticized [Second Life creator] Linden Labs [LL] for banning role-playing between consenting adults. Others pointed out that virtual killings occur frequently in Second Life and in games like World of Warcraft and that no one gets arrested for murder.

Explicit images of virtual children often indicate the presence of explicit images of real children.

One difference, however, is that explicit images of virtual children often indicate the presence of explicit images of real children. In the Second Life case, for instance, the allegations involve both rendered and actual images of children.

Chris Peterson, a writer for the satirical Web site SomethingAwful.com, said he's visited age-play areas in Second Life and was revolted by what he saw: "These were avatars of pre-pubescent children screaming in baby talk, 'Stop torturing me,' while individuals are doing unimaginable things. They're creating childish avatars that are four- or five-year-olds, and the sex acts are in a room covered with children's wallpaper," he said.

Other Second Life residents expressed skepticism about what they see as a face-saving move by Linden Labs. "Dozens of times in the past, LL employees themselves have come out on the community forums and publicly defended age-play as fantasy role-play between consenting adults," said someone posting under the name Charlotte Wirtanen. "Now suddenly everyone is pretending that they had no idea any of this was happening, when age-players are a massive, massive part of the SL user base."

Aftab believes that incidents like this may prompt social networks to adopt social policing through better reporting policies and procedures. She said that she's currently working with teen-oriented social site Xanga on better community reporting tools.

A Small Victory

The neighborhood watch is coming soon to the Internet near you. Monday [May 14, 2007] may bring a small victory for the government in its effort to curtail child pornography online. Aaron Campbell Brown of Boston, Mass., the alleged owner and operator of a Web hosting and payment processing company that facilitated trafficking in child pornography, is scheduled for a change of plea hearing, a spokesperson for the U.S. Attorney's Office in Roanoke, Virginia, confirmed on Friday [May 11, 2007]. Brown initially pleaded not guilty.

Brown is not expected to be sentenced immediately, in part so he can cooperate with the government, possibly in exchange for a reduced sentence, said a source familiar with the case.

The U.S. Attorney's Office in Roanoke declined to clarify any details about the plea agreement before it is officially disclosed next week [mid-May 2007].

Brown's decision to change his plea may have something to do with the substantial sentence received by the defendant in a related prosecution.

Last July [2006], Gregory John Mitchell of Dublin, Virginia was sentenced to 150 years in prison for the production, sale, distribution, and possession of child pornography. Mitchell allegedly used Brown's payment processing services.

In April [2007], Brown lost a motion to exclude the testimony of two computer forensic experts.

Child pornography remains a serious problem online, despite aggressive law enforcement efforts. The increasing popularity of social networking has only magnified the ways in which child pornography can be disseminated.

Real child porn is present on lots of social networks.

"Real child porn is present on lots of social networks," said Parry Aftab, an attorney, author, and executive director of

WiredSafety.org. "You can get images of children to download to your iPod. You can order a live online molestation of a real child for viewing."

And because there's so much child pornography online, law enforcement officials have to prioritize. "No one in law enforcement is really dealing with images," said Aftab, "because there are live kids being held captive."

Coming to Terms

That leaves social networks and virtual worlds like Second Life under policed. And while social networks and virtual worlds tend to be responsive to copyright infringement claims, they're not known for dealing well with other issues. "Rarely can I get blogs taken down for cyber-stalking or harassment," said Aftab. "Getting anyone at Blogger [a free Weblog site] to do anything is next to impossible."

But social sites are coming to terms with their responsibilities. Aftab said that she had recently chanced across obvious child pornography on a major social network. Because she's currently working with authorities on the issue, she declined to discuss further details.

On Wednesday [May 9, 2007], Second Life officials acknowledged banning a 54-year-old man and a 27-year-old woman from the virtual world after being presented with images showing the pair's avatars, one adult male and the other a child, engaged in sexual activity.

In a blog post, VP [vice president] of community and support Robin Harper, writing under the Second Life surname "Linden," said Linden Lab had been informed of the incident by a reporter from German television station ARD and that it had been told that images had been passed on to a state attorney in Halle, Germany. The company said it has tried unsuccessfully to contact German authorities.

Under German law, possession of virtual child pornography can result in a sentence of up to three years. Under U.S.

law, images qualify as child pornography if they depict or appear to depict a real child engaged in explicit activity. Illustrations or non-realistic renderings, however, such as those in Second Life, qualify for First Amendment protection, unless they are obscene.

"Linden Lab has absolutely zero tolerance for depictions of child pornography within Second Life," the company said. "We were outraged to see the images that ARD showed us, and will cooperate fully with any legal authorities that choose to investigate the individuals involved in such activities. Child pornography is, of course, illegal and as such is a breach of our Terms of Service."

The German television reporter Nick Shader [during his investigation] was reportedly asked to pay to attend meetings where both virtual and real child pornography were available.

8

MySpace Takes Measures to Safeguard Minors

Julia Angwin and Brian Steinberg

Julia Angwin and Brian Steinberg are staff reporters for the Wall Street Journal.

MySpace and its owner, media company News Corporation, aim to make MySpace a safer social networking Web site for teenagers. Because it is the largest social network and has a large number of users who are under seventeen, MySpace is criticized by parents, teachers, and law enforcement for exposing minors to risqué content and the increasing number of alleged sexual abuse cases involving its underage users. In response, MySpace contends that every user-loaded photo is checked for explicit content and that it screens for young users who lie about their ages. However, because it is a free Web site with a vast number of profiles, My-Space does not currently have the means to verify its users' ages.

When News Corp. bought the social-networking Web site MySpace.com last July [2005], the media company got two surprises, one good and one bad.

The good part: The site, where teens and twenty-somethings post pages about themselves and communicate with friends, already was popular, but it suddenly took off. In the last six months of 2005, MySpace's monthly traffic doubled to 36 million users, making it the eighth-most-visited Web site in January [2006], according to comScore Media Metrix [a company that tabulates search engine volume]. News Corp. Chairman Rupert Murdoch declared it the centerpiece of his new Internet strategy of attracting a large audience in a bid to bypass portals such as Yahoo Inc. and Microsoft Corp.'s MSN in advertising revenue.

The bad part: MySpace has become the focus of criticism from authorities, teachers and parents that children are exposed to risqué content and are preyed upon by sexual predators who meet them on the site. Such episodes aren't unique to MySpace, but the site stands out because of its size—54 million registered users, with about [22 percent] of monthly users under 17, according to [MySpace].

News Corp. is scrambling to make MySpace a safer place for young people.

In response, News Corp. is scrambling to make MySpace a safer place for young people. News Corp. plans to appoint a "safety czar" to oversee the site, launch an education campaign that may include letters to schools and public-service announcements to encourage children not to reveal their contact information. It also is considering limiting access to certain groups, such as "swingers," to those over 18; blocking search terms that predators could use to locate kids; and encouraging users between 14 and 16 to make their profiles "private," meaning they can only be viewed by people they already know.

"We're going to take some pretty dramatic steps to provide industry-leading safety," says Ross Levinsohn, president of News Corp.'s Fox Interactive Media unit, which includes MySpace.

A Delicate Operation

It is a delicate operation for News Corp. because the media group wants to retain MySpace's cool factor. Like other Web sites, MySpace owes its success largely to its freewheeling nature. If the site feels too supervised, teenagers could leave in droves. "MySpace was the first one to allow users to customize their pages any way they wanted," says Parry Aftab, a cybersecurity lawyer who advises MySpace. "That's why MySpace took off like it did."

Yet while many teens use MySpace to innocently chat with friends and share music, other MySpace users post sexually explicit photos and list activities such as "swinging" and "spanking" among their interests. The site has so many explicit pictures that Playboy Enterprises Inc. has launched a casting call for a "Girls of MySpace" nude pictorial for an upcoming issue of its magazine. "We've done a lot of these types of castings, and this is by far the best response we've gotten to date," says Michael Sprouse, senior vice president of marketing at Playboy. Playboy requires applicants to submit two forms of ID proving they are over 18. MySpace isn't affiliated with the contest and says it doesn't endorse it.

Sexual-abuse allegations involving MySpace are increasing. Police in Middletown, Conn., say they are investigating complaints that five men in their 20s posed as teens, contacted female MySpace users as young as 11 and eventually sexually assaulted them.

No one has been charged, "but we feel confident that we are going to get arrests out of it," says Sgt. Bill McKenna supervisor of the family-services unit of the Middletown Police Department. "Investigations of this nature just take a long time to get everything right."

In September, police in Port Washington, N.Y., arrested a 37-year-old man for allegedly molesting a 16-year-old girl he met on MySpace. This month, police in Bristol, Conn., arrested a 21-year-old for having sex with a minor whom he allegedly met on MySpace.

Connecticut Attorney General Richard Blumenthal said earlier this month that his office is investigating whether MySpace is doing enough to protect children from being contacted by predators and from viewing pornography. MySpace Chief Executive Chris DeWolfe and two News Corp. executives have met with Mr. Blumenthal, and while the attorney general says the meeting was encouraging he says MySpace's proposals don't go far enough. "We're going to be making some counterproposals that are more demanding," he says.

"It's a parent's worst nightmare to have a young person on this Web site dispensing all kinds of information," says Mr. Blumenthal. "You will not persuade me that they can't do a better job of it. Right now it's the Wild West." Mr. DeWolfe says MySpace is committed to working with Mr. Blumenthal to make the site safe and secure.

MySpace says it has employees who check each photo landed onto the site, although it says only a few are rejected, because users realize explicit material will be kicked out. Instead, MySpace says users often add a link to racy photos stored on other sites, such as PhotoBucket.com and ImageShack.us. PhotoBucket.com Chief Executive Alex Welch says his site is beefing up its photo-scanning capabilities so it can scan all the images and kick out explicit photos. ImageShack.us says it already scans all photos that are uploaded to its site to check for porn. MySpace competitor Facebook.com doesn't allow photos linked to image-hosting sites.

[MySpace] says it has a computer program that checks for clues that users might be lying about their ages and has removed 200,000 profiles as a result.

MySpace used to block access to those who said they were under the age of 16. But so many lied about their ages that MySpace lowered the age limit to 14—and blocked certain communication features for users between the ages of 14 and

16. The company says it has a computer program that checks for clues that users might be lying about their age and has removed 200,000 profiles as a result. Like other sites, MySpace doesn't verify users' ages. "No one on the Internet with a free site has ever come up with a way to do that," Mr. DeWolfe says.

Contending with Backlash

MySpace is also contending with backlash from advertisers, schools and parents. Some advertisers feel leery about the site—even though it reaches the much-coveted youth demographic. . . .

Middletown High School [in Connecticut] like other high schools and colleges, blocks its students' access to MySpace from school computers and plans a workshop for parents on how to manage their children's access to MySpace.

More parents are taking the initiative themselves. Bellrose, N.Y., resident Connie Couvertier recently shut down her 12-year-old daughter's MySpace profile and access to the site. Although her daughter's profile was an innocent listing of her interests and friends, Mrs. Couvertier says she was shocked by the other risqué profiles and photographs. Says her husband, Augustine: "It's just a sexually charged atmosphere that is inappropriate for young kids."

9

Schools Should Punish Students for Misuse of Networking Sites

Duff, White & Turner, LLC

Duff, White & Turner is a South Carolina–based law firm that represents business and educational institutions.

Although it takes place outside of school, harassment, delinquency, and misconduct on social networking Web sites such as MySpace can hurt students, teachers, and campus morale. Therefore, schools and districts should use their authority and legal power to prevent, intervene, and impose disciplinary sanctions against these incidents. Students who attempt to refute a reprimand or punishment may seek the First Amendment, or the freedom of speech, for protection. However, it is within the authority of schools and districts to discipline inappropriate behavior—online or off-campus—to maintain school safety and the well-being of students, teachers, and other school personnel.

As summer is in full swing and school employees are enjoying a much-deserved break from the daily school routine, administrators are grappling with the question of how to respond to challenges posed by the increasing popularity of

Duff, White & Turner, LLC, "The Internet and Public Schools: MySpace.com and Similar Websites Pose New Challenges for School Officials," *School Law Issue of the Month, www.ddtwb.com,* June 2006. Reproduced by permission. www.ddtwb.com/ November-2007/July2006.shtml.

social-networking Internet sites such as "MySpace.com" and "Facebook.com." These sites provide an opportunity for individuals, including students and school employees, to create their own webpage or weblog ("blog") on which they can share personal information and post or receive comments to/from other Internet users. In addition to raising broader safety concerns, most districts have learned that webpages have the potential to disrupt the school environment and/or adversely affect the morale of students and school employees.

Improper Use of Internet Sites

Schools around the country, including those in South Carolina, have dealt with a number of incidents concerning the improper use of Internet sites. While some incidents have involved district-owned computers, the majority involved conduct that took place off campus and through the use of personal computers. For example, in Libertyville, Illinois, after several students posted threatening comments about other students on the Internet during off-school hours on their home computers, the school board amended its student code of conduct to ban "illegal or inappropriate" behavior involving threats against students on the Internet, and subjecting violators to disciplinary action. In Missouri, several male high school students were suspended for 10 days after they posted on the Facebook Website, from their home computer, derogatory comments about female students attending their school. A high school senior in Pennsylvania also was suspended from school after he posted an unflattering parody of his school principal on MySpace. Finally, school officials in Winthrop, Massachusetts, suspended and recommended the expulsion of a student who had posted a "hate list" of other students on his MySpace page, along with a photo of a masked person carrying guns.

In addition to the problems posed by student use of the Internet, the proliferation of MySpace pages also has created new challenges in the area of school personnel. For example, in one South Carolina school district, a principal learned that one of her teachers had posted suggestive comments in response to student photographs on a student's MySpace page.

In considering how schools may legally respond to these and other instances of Internet misuse, school officials should keep in mind their broad authority to implement rules governing student conduct, whether that conduct occurs on school grounds and/or during school hours, or away from the school campus. Section 59-63-210 of the South Carolina Education Code authorizes school trustees to expel, suspend, or transfer any pupil, not only for "the commission of any crime, gross immorality, gross misbehavior, persistent disobedience, or for violation of written rules and promulgated regulations" but also when "the presence of [that student] is detrimental to the best interest of the school." This statutory authority permits a school to impose disciplinary sanctions where a student engages in inappropriate off-campus conduct, such as posting online comments which harass or threaten other students or staff members, or which otherwise negatively impacts the school environment. In such cases, the student may argue that the school has no authority to discipline for off-campus behavior, or that his/her actions are protected by the First Amendment. However, provided the school can demonstrate that the student's off-campus conduct has resulted in a material disruption of the school environment, the school may lawfully discipline the student for such behavior.

To ensure students and parents understand that districts may impose disciplinary sanctions for off-campus behavior involving inappropriate use of the Internet, districts should implement Computer/Internet Acceptable Use Policies. These policies should not only put students on notice concerning the appropriate use of District-owned technology, but also advise students that posting harassing, threatening or otherwise inappropriate comments on MySpace, Facebook, or other such Websites, is disrupting to the school, and may lead to disciplinary action.

The Internet and a secure school environment need not be mutually exclusive.

Maintaining a Safe and Secure School Environment

Concerning a district's right to discipline school employees for off-campus computer activity, districts should keep in mind both the provisions of the S.C. [South Carolina] Teacher Employment and Dismissal Act setting forth the grounds for which certified employees may be dismissed, as well as the school board policies that enumerate the expectations for employee conduct. The Employment and Dismissal Act provides that a certified employee may be dismissed for conduct evidencing an "unfitness for teaching," which includes, among other things, "willful violation of rules and regulations of district board of trustees . . . conviction of a violation of the law of this State or the United States, gross immorality, [and] dishonesty. . . ." Districts should implement staff conduct policies which clearly place employees on notice that, while their personal life generally is not the concern of the district, any conduct, including off-campus behavior, which results in a school disruption, or otherwise negatively impacts on the employee's credibility, can serve as the basis for discipline, up to and including termination. In addition, all employees should be required to sign a Computer/Internet Acceptable Use policy which notifies employees that off-campus computer use which adversely affects the school environment can result in discipline.

The Internet, with all of its information-gathering abilities, is a useful tool for students and school employees that no school district would want to eliminate. However, it also can present challenges in maintaining a safe and secure school environment. Provided districts take precautionary steps to minimize potential problems, the Internet and a secure school environment need not be mutually exclusive.

10

Punishing Students for Their Activities on Web Sites Is Inappropriate

Maggie Thompson

Maggie Thompson is a former reporter for the Campanile, *a student newspaper started in 1931 at Palo Alto High School in Palo Alto, California.*

Unless students use MySpace and other online social networks to threaten other students, teachers, and campus safety, schools should not punish them for posting negative comments or photos of inappropriate off-campus behavior. Schools that punish students for freely expressing their opinions online infringe on the students' First Amendment rights. Furthermore, disciplining them for off-campus behavior is an unjustified extension of campus authority. Instead, disciplinary action and limitations should be left to the individual's parents or legal guardians, and schools should educate students on the potential risks of social networking and the Internet.

Recent events have brought Internet websites such as www .MySpace.com, www.Facebook.com and www.Web shots.com under scrutiny for putting teenagers into vulnerable situations.

MySpace and Facebook are popular websites through which members post pictures and information and communi-

Maggie Thompson, "Student Freedom of Expression under Illegal Scrutiny," *Campanile*, March 14, 2006. Reproduced by permission. http://voice.paly.net/view_story .php?id=4017.

cate with other users. The information, messages and photographs are usually accessible to anyone who is a member. Webshots allows members to post pictures and grants access to even non-members.

With the attention and controversy surrounding these popular Internet websites, schools all over the country, from the Bay Area to Rhode Island, have been getting involved in the issue of Internet safety.

The controversy over MySpace and other similar sites brings up an important question: when is school involvement appropriate, and when is it not?

Palo Alto High School [in California] and all other schools reserve the right to punish students if something they have placed on the web is clearly dangerous or threatening to their peers. The right of schools to educate and to maintain a safe and growth-promoting community is undeniable.

The primary function of any school is to educate its students, regardless of what that education entails. As a place for learning, Paly [Palo Alto High School] as well as all schools, has every right to educate its students on Internet safety.

But in many other situations involving MySpace, schools' rights to involvement and rights to take disciplinary actions are not obvious and often controversial.

At schools throughout the country, students are being suspended for comments posted about their school and peers, or pictures showing illegal or inappropriate things such as under-age drinking.

Schools should not punish students for comments posted online about their schools, even if the comments are negative. Unless the comments threaten the safety or comfort of fellow students or school faculty, intervention is simply a violation of a student's freedom of speech, punishing the student for his or her public opinions.

In a recent case at Littleton High School in Littleton, Colorado, a junior was suspended for comments he posted about his school. The American Civil Liberties Union threatened to sue the school on the grounds that the school was violating the student's right to freedom of speech, protected under the First Amendment to the United States Constitution.

Crossing the Line

Schools have the right and duty to protect students and staff from online bullying and potentially dangerous threats, but beyond that, suspension for students' comments on the Internet is simply a violation of the right to freedom of speech and expression.

In other cases, such as at East Senior High School in Mankato, Minnesota, students were suspended from extra-curricular activities for posting pictures of themselves participating in underage drinking.

Twenty students at East Grand Rapids High School [in Michigan] were suspended from sporting events and the school dance for posting pictures online of themselves drinking alcohol at parties. None of these parties took place on school grounds.

In these cases, schools are punishing students for actions and behaviors taking place outside of school, something that should be left up to the parents of these individuals to handle.

By suspending students for their activities or comments that don't directly threaten students at a school or the atmosphere of learning at the school, administrators are abusing their authority.

Posting pictures online of oneself participating in underage drinking or illegal activities is certainly not a smart idea, but by choosing to punish students for these actions outside of school, schools are crossing the line between a student's school life and home life.

Some schools are going so far as to ban students from using MySpace and other Internet blog websites.

In Rhode Island, school districts are blocking student use of MySpace. According to Rhode Island Network for Education Technology, 80 percent of school departments are banning www.MySpace.com.

At Pope John XXIII High School in New Jersey, students are suspended if caught using MySpace, at school or at home.

Schools have every right to limit students' use of www.MySpace.com while on campus; while at school students should be concentrated on learning.

But at home, it is up to the individual guardians of the students to set limitations.

Students have the right to privacy to do what they want at their home without the 24-hour surveillance by school administrators.

Schools can and should educate students about the risks they are taking when joining online websites such as www.MySpace.com and the consequences of posting pictures and comments online. But by suspending students for their activities or comments that don't directly threaten students at a school or the atmosphere of learning at the school, administrators are abusing their authority. Rather than spending time singling students out and "teaching them a lesson" for their foolish actions, school administrators and teachers should take advantage of the wonderful opportunity they have to do what they do best: educate.

11

Social Networking Web Sites Are Beneficial to Children and Teens

Jan Farrington

Jan Farrington is a writer for Current Health 2, *a health magazine for young adults.*

Contrary to several prevailing assumptions, MySpace and other social networking Web sites on the whole benefit the children and teenagers who use them. These sites help young people create and maintain lifelong connections with others and give them a sense of community. Additionally, while children and teenagers on MySpace and similar Web sites face potential risks and problems, most use online communities to engage in their real-life friendships, not to communicate with strangers. Finally, social networking Web sites are places where young people are judged on their personalities rather than superficial characteristics.

Did you know that MySpace has more than 100 million users? Okay, you're not shocked. Ninety percent of U.S. 12- to 17-year-olds say they go online. Whether they use MySpace or Xanga, instant messaging (IM) or e-mail (how last century is that?), teens spend a lot of time linked in cyberspace. What do social-networking sites really do for American teens? Does the online world affect face-to-face friendships—or is it just as good as the "real thing"? You might be surprised at what *Current Health* found out!

Marcus R., a 14-year-old from Springfield, Ill., loves online role-playing games—where he operates in "realms" populated by thousands of other players. But, he says, he likes to take some of his real-world friends along with him. "It isn't as much fun unless you can talk to someone you know," says Marcus.

Lauren B., 17, from Arlington, Texas, attends a high school "so big my friends and I never see each other during the day. So we IM everybody after school."

Young people desperately need community, and a community in cyberspace can be a tremendous help and outlet.

"It's so easy for teens to stay connected—and that's a great thing," says Patricia Hersch, the author of *A Tribe Apart*. She is currently working on a book about teens' strong need for connection with others. With busy schedules and long distances making face-to-face time rare, Hersch says, "young people desperately need community, and a community in cyberspace can be a tremendous help and outlet."

Hanging (Online) with Friends: It Can Be Good for You!

If it all disappeared one day—IM and Facebook, MySpace and e-mail—would you care? "It would be a pretty big deal to me," says Mike L., a 13-year-old from Elmhurst, Ill. He uses IM to keep in touch with local pals and friends from his old school in England.

Mike is pretty typical, say researchers at Carnegie Mellon University. They found that most teens spend the bulk of their time online keeping up with real-life friends, not talking to strangers in chat rooms (which many think are "a waste of time," the study found).

Researchers say IM is an especially useful tool. It gives teens an easy way to keep in touch with a small group of "core" friends while letting them hang out with a wider social circle. Teens seem to need both types of friendships.

Two years ago, Lauren J., 16, moved from Texas to Severna Park, Md., leaving behind her best friend and a big circle of buddies. Now she's moving back to Texas and says that because of "IM and MySpace and Yahoo Messenger, it's like I never really was gone." Without online communication, she says, "I wouldn't have felt as happy and connected, and it would have been way harder to be away from my friends. But my best friend back home is still my best friend—and now I have friends in Maryland to IM too!"

Still, life online isn't always friendly. "There's a lot of gossip," says Lauren B. "One of my friends was looking at somebody else's MySpace [profile] and found comments about her. [That person] denied it, but the words were there, and [my friend] was really upset."

Problems or quarrels that begin in the real world are often "kept up" online, she adds—and it can be easy to get excited and "sound too mean" about somebody in an IM or a MySpace comment. Lauren B. thinks if there's trouble with real-life friends, teens should try to handle it face-to-face: "It's more sincere to break up with a guy or apologize for something important in person, not with an IM."

Online, kids are judged by their ideas.

Still, Hersch says that in tough situations the Internet becomes a place where teens can explore their feelings and talk honestly about events in the world and in their lives. "Young people often express a level of emotion that they never would have expressed face-to-face with each other," she told *Current Health*.

Parry Aftab, the executive director of WiredSafety.org, also believes that the online world has a lot to offer. "This is a place where teens can really be who they are," she says. "Online, kids are judged by their ideas," not by who has the hottest body or the coolest car.

"One of the fabulous things about the internet is that no matter where you live, it can put you together with people who share your special interests or situation. . . . It enlarges your community and lets you know you're not alone," Aftab notes.

When to Be Careful

Still, says Aftab, teens need to be cautious even when they think they're talking to their real-life friends. "You can't ever know for sure who you're talking to online," agrees Lauren J. "It might be some other person pretending to be your friend. So you try not to say things you wouldn't want other people to [know]."

She and her friends are quick to take action when something doesn't seem right. "One time, a girl who wasn't really a friend of mine told me in an IM that she was going to have somebody beat up one of my best friends," says Lauren. "That was a big deal! I printed off the instant message and turned it in at the school office—and that stopped it."

Never be afraid to back out of a situation online, block unwanted communications, or report bullying or hurtful comments.

You Have Got Connections

Parents say they worry that the online world is taking over teen social life. But here's the reality: A 2005 Pew Research Center survey found that though 12- to 17-year-olds spent 7.8 hours a week connecting to friends online, they spent even more time face-to-face. That's an average of 10.3 hours of social activity with friends (outside school) per week!

What's more, teens plan to stay connected to their friends through college—and maybe forever. Unlike your parents and grandparents, you will have a much easier time keeping in touch with a lifetime's worth of people you know and care about, no matter where you go. If you avoid trouble spots, the online world gives you a real opportunity to spend even more time, now and in the years ahead, with some very important people in your life: your friends!

Caught in the Net?

Keeping Yourself Safe Online.

However fun and interesting the online world can seem, you need to be safe. Parry Aftab, the executive director of WiredSafety.org, says there's a lot you can do to protect yourself. She calls it learning to use "the filter between your ears"—your brain! Here's her best advice.

- "Have fun, learn things, talk to people—but understand that people you meet online are not real-life friends."

- "Don't tell secrets to someone you met online."

- "Recognize that there are many adults online posing as teens—more of them than teens like to think."

- "Don't tell your personal stuff. You can't really know who that online person really is."

- "Have a cyberbuddy—a good friend who will look over your online communications and tell you when something doesn't feel right, or who can look at your profile on MySpace and say, 'Change that.'"

Discuss.

- With whom do teens spend most of their online time interacting? (real-life friends, not strangers in chat rooms)

- What are the advantages of online communication? (It helps teens find connection and a sense of community; enables teens to stay in touch with both local and distant friends; and provides a way for teens to talk about their true feelings and be themselves.)

- What problems can teens encounter online? (hurtful gossip and meanness, strangers who pose as friends or other teens, and harassment)

- Which strategy do you think works best for maintaining friendships: instant messages, social-network Web sites such as MySpace, e-mail, phone calls, or text messages? Why? (Answers will vary.)

Do.

Most of today's teens are savvy about online perils, but younger kids may not understand the dangers. Have students write a series of skits that illustrate ways to stay safe online. They can use the tips in the article, material from other online-safety Web sites, and their own experiences. Ask for volunteer actors, and present the skits for younger children in your school or community.

12

The Military Has Legitimate Reasons to Ban Social Networking Web Sites

Erika Morphy

Erika Morphy is a technology reporter.

In May 2007 the U.S. Department of Defense prohibited access to MySpace, YouTube, and other social networking Web sites on military networks, and troops now are allowed to access these Web sites only on nonmilitary networks. The motivations of this ban are legitimate: Social networking and Internet video Web sites use up bandwidth and have slowed down military networks, which are constantly threatened by enemy hackers and invaders. Furthermore, this ban prevents the real-time location of U.S. vessels from being revealed and protects military networks from computer viruses. Blocking access to these Web sites takes an emotional toll on troops and their families and friends, but alternative social networks are available for their use.

Citing limited bandwidth and potential security issues, the Pentagon has cut off U.S. troops' access to several social networking and other high-volume Web sites. Soldiers can still post to MySpace and YouTube—two of the banned sites—but only from outside networks.

However, most overseas military personnel, including thousands stationed in Iraq and Afghanistan, have no Internet

Erika Morphy, *TechNewsWorld*, "What's Motivating the Military's Selective Web Site Ban?" *TechNewsWorld*, May 15, 2007. Reproduced by permission. www.technewsworld.com/story/57400.html.

access other than the Defense Department networks, which they rely on to stay in touch with family and friends.

Other sites covered by the ban include Metacafe, IFilm, StupidVideos, FileCabi, BlackPlanet, Hi5, Pandora, MTV, 1.fm, live365 and Photobucket.

Legitimate Concerns

To be sure, bandwidth requirements pose a legitimate concern that is not limited to the U.S. military. Large corporations, for instance, have taken to locking employees out of popular streaming video sites at the workplace in order to ensure that their networks can run at full capacity.

Sharing videos, swapping photos and other popular Web 2.0 activities can easily eat up a lot of bandwidth, said Jeff Stibel, CEO [chief executive officer] of Web.com, which provides military families with tools to create multimedia sites.

"It can be a concern," he told *TechNewsWorld*.

Also, security risks should not be underestimated, warns Melissa Feagin, a former information systems technician who recently separated from the U.S. Navy.

"A military network is an entirely different entity than a civilian one," she told *TechNewsWorld*.

Every day, our networks are under attack from foreign invaders.

"Every day, our networks are under attack from foreign invaders. Whoever thinks our enemies are out herding their camels are sadly mistaken. Our militant enemies have networks of very intelligent, trained operatives working night and day to hack into our networks."

Although the military warns sailors and soldiers to never reveal their schedules or locations, "there will inevitably always be that one who does tell his mom back in Wisconsin that 'the ship is pulling into Dubai next Tuesday,'" Feagin continued. "Especially after the USS *Cole* tragedy [in which a U.S. Navy destroyer was attacked by two suicide bombers while in port in Yemen in October 2000], mistakes like this can be deadly."

MySpace has a feature called "MySpace Chat," she noted. "Any chat space online allowing users real-time conversation is strictly forbidden on board United States Navy vessels, as that mistake that one person lets slip out may reveal the ship's exact real-time location."

By blocking access to such sites, the Pentagon is also protecting itself from a common virus vector, Dan Nadir, vice president of product strategy for ScanSafe, told *TechNewsWorld*. "Some users are not that sophisticated in knowing not to download certain files from a P2P (peer-to-peer) site, for example," he said. "This is a valid security risk—not only in the military, but in the corporate world as well."

Moment to moment

Still, the ban—which the Pentagon imposed with little warning—is undercutting a type of communications near and dear to deployed armed forces and their families. Soldiers have been using these sites to stay in touch and give their loved ones some sense of what is happening with them.

"Real-time communication is so important in these situations," Andi Hurley, founder of Spousebuzz.com, a Web site for military spouses, told *TechNewsWorld*. "It empowers military families—and we are exploiting it for all that it is worth."

Hurley, whose husband was deployed in Afghanistan, told of a recent military spouses' convention she recently attended. "We talked about how difficult—inconceivable, actually—it must have been for spouses in World War II or Vietnam, waiting weeks and weeks for a letter. Being able to see your spouse and talk directly—virtual or otherwise—makes all the difference at the home front."

Alternative Mode

In response to the military's dictum, sites such as Web.com and WebsitesforHeroes.com are likely to become more trafficked as overseas personnel seek to stay in touch. These sites use various means to minimize bandwidth usage.

In the case of Web.com, it avoids social networking and linkages that can slow systems.

WebsitesforHeroes.com employs a compression technology that "shrinks" photos as they're uploaded to a standard size, thus reducing the strain on the system. These sites typically come with password-protected technology to satisfy the Pentagon's security concerns.

That is assuming, of course, that the military wants its personnel to be using these sites at all—regardless of whether they are safe or easy on the network.

One dark suspicion that's making the rounds in the blogosphere is that the Pentagon wishes to shut down any communication by the troops that may reflect unfavorably on what is happening in Iraq.

The move to ban the social networking and photo-sharing sites follows a far more onerous ban on personal communications implemented earlier this year.

E-mail Monitoring

Reportedly, the army has recently ordered soldiers to stop writing blogs or sending personal e-mail messages, unless the content has been cleared by a superior officer. These new regs [regulations], which can be punishable by court martial or criminal action if violated, also apply to spouses and friends, although jurisdiction is unclear on that point.

For some military personnel, the restrictions have been hard to swallow.

The new regulation "does not distinguish between on-duty, off-duty, deployed, non-deployed, military computers, personal computers, etc.," writes one solider.

"In effect, it dictates to me, my family and my friends that they cannot send e-mail or publish their own blogs, regardless of content. So, technically, every time my wife wants to send an e-mail, she needs to get permission from my commander or OPSEC (operations security) officer beforehand. While the intent is geared towards the release of OPSEC-related material, the reality is that the regulation effectively targets *every* form of electronic communication utilized by Soldiers *and* their family members."

The Electronic Frontier Foundation (EFF) has filed a lawsuit against the Department of Defense, demanding information on how the Army monitors soldiers' blogs. Even before the new regulations went into effect, there were accounts of an Army unit called the "Army Web Risk Assessment Cell" (AWRAC) that reportedly reviewed hundreds of thousands of Web sites every month, notifying webmasters and bloggers of information it found inappropriate.

"Soldiers should be free to blog their thoughts at this critical point in the national debate on the war in Iraq," said EFF Staff Attorney Marcia Hofmann.

"If the Army is coloring or curtailing soldiers' published opinions, Americans need to know about that interference."

In light of the military's most recent action, Americans certainly won't learn about it at MySpace or other familiar Internet haunts.

13

The Military Ban on Social Networking Web Sites Lowers Morale

Todd Garvin

Todd Garvin is a writer for the Glasgow Daily Times *in Glasgow, Kentucky.*

Individuals serving in the armed forces make great sacrifices to serve their country, and the U.S. Department of Defense's ban on MySpace and other social networking Web sites heavily affects troops' morale. If blocking access to these Web sites is a security issue, troops should be carefully trained on the appropriate use of the Internet when communicating with their friends and family instead. Men and women serving in the war in Iraq face real threats to their lives everyday, and allowing them small joys like keeping in touch with their families and other "tastes of home" is crucial to their well-being.

Imagine a world where every step you take will be your last. A world where you are despised, despite the fact your very presence is to ensure the safety of those who detest you. A world where bullets and bombs are as commonplace as fast food eateries on the corners of our country. Sadly, thousands of Americans don't have to imagine such a place—they live in it.

The members of our armed forces dutifully perform the tasks set before them on a daily basis despite the barrage of

Todd Garvin, "MySpace Ban Will Affect Soldiers' Morale," *Glasgow Daily Times*, May 19, 2007. Reproduced by permission. http://www.glasgowdailytimes.com/opinion/local_story_139112412.html?keyword=secondarystory.

dangers and degradation that come their way. They do it away from their homeland . . . their friends . . . their families. Although their lives are on the line every day, soldiers are now forbidden to be online for certain Web sites that simplify communication with loved ones back home concerned for their well-being.

The military's decision to block access to sites such as You-Tube and MySpace makes about as much sense as attacking Madagascar. The Pentagon cites one reason for the denial of Web access as security. Although one could make an argument that an online video might tip the enemy off to troop positions, do military officials really expect us to believe that militants and terrorists aren't tracking that information with intelligence other than Google?

Besides, it's highly doubtful that the men and women of the armed services are posting things such as, "Hey, Mom. Can't type long today because we're attacking the third house from the northeast corner on Habib Street at 5:17 p.m. with 13 riflemen and an M1 Abrams and Apache attack helicopter in support."

Allowing these men and women to have an avenue for reaching family back home seems a very small price to pay for the service and sacrifice they give daily.

All the More Questionable

Another reason for not allowing access to certain sites was bandwidth, or the transmission capacity of a network. So, fix it. It's really that simple . . . or at least it should be.

Allowing these men and women to have an avenue for reaching family back home seems a very small price to pay for the service and sacrifice they give daily.

Common sense dictates that even the smallest form of frequent "tastes of home" cut down on the stress related with being in harm's way. A healthy and clear mind is crucial for our fighting men and women as they face the dangers associated with protecting the helpless overseas.

Military officials could make a poignant argument that troops undergo training to prepare them for such hardships. However, those same units also are trained on ensuring security of certain materials and themselves.

If this training is being done properly, why would there be a need to restrict these Web sites?

One also cannot forget the hardship this ban will bring to those at home. Scores of mothers, wives and children will no longer be able to receive frequent pictures or videos of loved ones fighting half the globe away.

Sure, the military has not banned e-mail. However, most e-mail servers cannot handle lengthy video or large pictures as easily—if at all—as the now-blocked Web sites.

Also, MySpace and YouTube allow those in the military to reach all their friends and loved ones at one time, even new people who might want to offer words of encouragement and support. You can even watch music videos of [actress and singer] Jennifer Love Hewitt, which is good for anyone's morale.

History teaches us that morale is vital to armies protecting their own lands or those of allies. That makes the reasoning of these bans all the more questionable.

In a world where Americans are dying daily, we need to be looking for ways to improve the quality of life for those men and women, not pulling the plug on one of the few perks they enjoy.

14

Social Networking Sites Benefit the Political Process

Christian Science Monitor

The Christian Science Monitor *is an international daily newspaper, started in 1908 by Church of Christ, Scientist, founder Mary Baker Eddy. The* Monitor *has writers based in eleven countries, including Russia, China, France, the United Kingdom, Kenya, Mexico, Israel, and India, as well as throughout the United States.*

As Internet connectors such as Facebook and Myspace continue to gain in popularity, they are beginning to be used beyond their inital purpose of allowing people to meet and connect with friends. One of the uses that has developed is the increased interest in political action, especially among young people. Analysts see an upsurge not only in the run-up to the 2008 presidential election in the United States, but also worldwide as political organizers in countries such as Venezuela and Colombia use social networking sites to mobilize voters.

The hottest Web innovations—social network sites—are swiftly shaping the way the world works, perhaps for the better. Their ability to create trust among strangers, mainly young people, is being used to mobilize political action, unexpectedly so in the American presidential campaign.

Social Networking Expands Beyond Connecting With Friends

Facebook, as well as other Internet connectors such as Twitter and "widgets," are being used beyond their original intent of simply finding and connecting friends. They are also a barrier-lowering technology that can bring a viral virility to organizing the masses.

They produce shared enthusiasm among the wired millions, creating a new consensus about the future. They can trigger an open subversion of powerful institutions and political elites, helping to level society.

[Social networking sites] generate "trust communities" that can grow quickly.

And they've proved far more effective than e-mail (which helped launch Howard Dean's brief candidacy in the 2004 Democratic contest) or recorded phone calls from candidates. And along with YouTube, this networking may overturn television's half-century of dominance in shaping opinion.

The big difference: They generate "trust communities" that can grow quickly.

Social Networking Increases Voter Turnout

In the Feb. 5 [2008] Super Tuesday primaries [when twenty states held primary elections], for instance, the use of Facebook by students helped create a stunning turnout of young people, not only at the ballot box but in that old-fashioned tactic of knocking on doors for candidates.

Compared with the 2000 contests, the number of voters under 30 was double in Massachusetts, triple in Georgia, Missouri, and Oklahoma, and quadruple in Tennessee. An estimated 14 percent of voters in the Democratic primaries have been 18-29 years old, up from 9 percent in 2004 and 8 percent back in 2000.

Much of this iPodic youthquake among the Millennials [people born between 1980 and 1995] was driven by the candidacy of Barack Obama. His oratory and relative youth drive many young people to the polls. In a new measure of political clout, the number of Mr. Obama's "friends" on Facebook and MySpace is far larger than for other candidates. The networks only accelerate his appeal.

This 21st-century digital democracy makes the Democrats' reliance on unelected "superdelegates" for picking a candidate seem like a throwback to smoke-filled back rooms.

Facebook represents freedom for people who use it for a cause.

Networking Sites Promote Freedom Worldwide

Another stunning use of Facebook occurred Feb. 4 in Colombia, a nation with little history of mass demonstrations. A group of young people used the website to organize hundreds of thousands for a one-day, worldwide protest against the kidnappings of Colombians and foreigners by that country's leftist rebels. The effect was a public cry against an imposition of fear.

The Internet's tools were also effectively used by about 120,000 Venezuelan students to mobilize the poor to vote against President Hugo Chávez in a Dec. 2 referendum aimed at enhancing his powers. The students were spurred into action last May after Mr. Chávez closed an independent television station. They also helped prevent Chávez's attempt at ballot fraud.

Facebook represents freedom for people who use it for a cause. Like any technology, though, the way it is used will determine if it is a force for good.

15

Social Networking Sites Draw Young People to Politics

Alexandra Marks

Alexandra Marks is a New York–based staff writer for the Christian Science Monitor.

In the run-up to the 2008 presidential election in the United States, political analysts noted a marked increase in the number of young people involved in the political process. Whether a backlash to the cynicism of the previous generation or dissatisfaction with the direction the country was heading during the George W. Bush administration, record numbers of young people voice concern for the future and are working to make a positive difference. One of the most effective tools in this surge is online networking. The ease with which young people utilize this new technology has contributed to the rise of its use by such groups as Rock the Vote and Vote Poke who are looking to engage more young people in the political process.

If politically active 20-somethings have their way, 2008 is going to be their year.

The "Millennials," [people born between 1980 and 1995] as sociologists have dubbed them, have already shaken up the presidential primary races with their surprisingly large turnouts in the Iowa caucuses and the New Hampshire primary at 13 percent and 43 percent respectively.

Political analysts are watching to see whether that increase in youth turnout holds when the politicking shifts from the retail-style handshaking in smaller states to the wholesale media buys and tarmac touchdowns in larger ones on Super Tuesday.

More Young People Are Voting

That's Feb. 5 [2008], when more than 20 states will hold primaries. If more young people turn out then, it could be the cementing of a trend started in 2000 when youth turnout started ticking upward. If you believe young people themselves, it is the beginning of a new brand of less cynical political engagement in the future.

"Super Tuesday puts the trend of higher youth involvement to the test," says Donald Green, a political scientist at Yale University in New Haven, Conn. "It forces us to explain the high voter turn out as either in terms of voter mobilization [which is easier in small states] or because of enthusiasm inspired by the candidates."

Talk to young people, and they have another reason as well: optimism. While "Gen-Xers" [people born between approximately 1960 and 1982] are known for their cynical alienation, these Millennials are socially active, engaged in volunteerism and determined to make the world a better place.

Caring About the Future

"Something is going on, that era of irony is finally playing itself out," says Marc Morgenstern, executive director of Declare Yourself, a nonpartisan youth voter mobilization organization in Los Angeles. "Cynicism and irony can only go so far. Eventually the pendulum has to swing the other way and it becomes cool again to care about things."

You can hear that in the voices of the young people who go to campaign events. In Las Vegas at a rally headlined by former President Clinton for his wife, Hillary Rodham Clinton, . . . Jalon Sisson said politics is personal for him.

"It's my future," said the young Las Vegas resident. "What I really don't understand is why there aren't more young people here because . . . we are the ones who are going to have to live with the problems of the future."

His friend Jarrell Roberts echoed another sentiment heard from many young people. It's a sense that the country hasn't been led well in their political lifetime, and they'd like to change that. "We just know from facts that President Bill Clinton was a way better president than President Bush," he says.

Young People Want the Truth

At an event for Barack Obama in Pahrump, Nev., another theme emerged: a desire among the young for the unvarnished truth.

Voter mobilization groups like Declare Yourself and Rock the Vote are using [social networking sites] to demystify the political process, from registration to issues explanation.

"Even if [there comes a time when] we won't like to hear what he says, he'll still tell you the truth," says Claire Chase.

Despite all the enthusiasm, political analysts note that since 1972 young voters have been notoriously unreliable. Just ask Howard Dean, the former governor of Vermont who staked his 2004 presidential bid on the youth vote only to be knocked out as a contender early in Iowa. Even with Mr. Dean's loss, more young people voted in 2004 than in 2000.

Here's a snapshot of what's been going on with young people ages 18 to 29 since 1972, according to The Center for Information & Research on Civic Learning & Engagement (CIRCLE). That year the Vietnam War and the draft prompted 55 percent of young people to come out and pull a lever for the candidate of their choice.

Then came Watergate and the youth turnout steadily declined for two decades, bottoming out at 40 percent in 1996 and 2000. It ticked up again when Bill Clinton first ran for president in 1992, but then dropped back down until 2000. Since then, at least for presidential elections, an increasing number of young people have come out to vote.

"We certainly are seeing something going on with young people," says Thomas Patterson, a political scientist at Harvard University's Kennedy School of Government. "If you're making a list of the things you'd like to [attribute] for the shift, Iraq is by far at the top of the list—George Bush is second."

"Young people are also pioneering new online tools to connect up with other folks."

Networking Sites Help Demystify Politics

The fact that both parties have active presidential campaigns with open races also helps, says Professor Patterson. Then there's technology. The Millennials are the wired generation, the scions of Facebook and MySpace social-networking websites. Voter mobilization groups like Declare Yourself and Rock the Vote are using them to demystify the political process, from registration to issues explanation. Each organization also hopes to register 2 million new young voters by the general election in November.

"Young people are also pioneering new online tools to connect up with other folks," says Karlo Marcelo, a researcher at CIRCLE at the University of Maryland in College Park. "I just saw this really neat tool called Vote Poke. You can enter in the name and address of a friend of yours and find out if they're registered to vote. If not, you can send them a note, saying 'Here's how you register online.' There are such simple things you can do now."

Despite the activity, young Americans still vote at lower levels than their older siblings, parents, and grandparents. But

Mr. Marcelo and others are optimistic that this could be the year that changes and young people pass the 50 percent mark and close the gap with older generations.

"This could be the third election in a row that we've increased youth turnout," says Chrissy Faessen, a spokeswoman for Rock the Vote in Washington. "It's pretty exciting."

But that excitement extends only on the presidential and congressional levels, according to analysts. In local elections turnout has been "abysmal," particularly for the young. "They've become selective shoppers: they believe presidential politics is worth their time—the rest of it, not so much," says Patterson.

16

Social Networking Sites Encourage Philanthropy

Christian Science Monitor

The Christian Science Monitor *is an international daily newspaper, started in 1908 by Church of Christ, Scientist, founder Mary Baker Eddy. The* Monitor *has writers based in eleven countries, including Russia, China, France, the United Kingdom, Kenya, Mexico, Israel, and India, as well as throughout the United States.*

Analysts have determined that the young people of today— dubbed "Millenials"—are more socially active than their "Generation X" predecessors. They volunteer more and are increasingly invested in making the world a better place. Politicians, and now charitiable organizations, picked up on the intersection of these young people with new technologies such as the Internet and cell phones and are using these technologies to draw more and more young people in. Charities are benefiting from social networking tools such as Facebook as young people spread the word about their own special causes and inspire support in others.

Charities know that young people volunteer. Over 90 percent of college-bound high school seniors have done community service—partly to be attractive to colleges, but partly out of goodwill. How to turn that goodwill into donations and foster a habit of financial giving? Technology can help.

Young people are connected to each other in ways that their parents weren't. The same bonds are there, but they are facilitated and widened by the Internet and cell-phones. Combine that with awareness of events, such as hurricane Katrina and the Pakistan earthquake in 2005, and the potential for financial support is significant.

Politicians discovered the intersection of technology and youth in the last presidential election cycle, and now they turn to it in fundraising. Campaigns attract small donations over the Internet from many people—especially from enthused, Web-savvy 20- and 30-somethings. In the end, that adds up to big bucks.

Internet Charitable Giving on the Rise

Now nonprofits are starting to catch on. They're not only providing a link on their Web pages for click-on donations, they're beginning to join with social-networking sites such as Facebook. There, friends can tell friends about their special causes and inspire support.

One charity experimenting with Facebook and other Internet fundraising facilitators is the Case Foundation, the private foundation of AOL founder Steve Case. In mid-December, it launched a fundraising drive to encourage people who may never have thought of themselves as donors to use the Internet to give at least $10 to their favorite charity—and to encourage friends and family to do the same.

The Internet and young givers are a natural match.

Case is making $750,000 available in grants to the charities. It will give up to $50,000 to the charities with the most donors who encourage the most people to give to their cause—that is, it's rewarding the building of the giving network itself, not just the amount donated.

The technology outreach is even touching elementary school kids. Over the holidays, 2.5 million children who play on the popular Club Penguin site (owned by Walt Disney), donated virtual coins earned by their virtual penguins. Club Penguin turned the play donations into a real gift of $1 million, dividing it among three major charities based on the children's preferences.

Parents, too, are using technology to instill the giving spirit in their offspring. They can now purchase "give cards," sold by such nonprofits as globalgiving.com, that allow people to visit their website, select charities around the world, and donate.

Charitable Organizations Have Concerns

The intersection of technology with young donors, however, is not without concern in the philanthropy world.

Some question whether the ease and fashion of electronic donating can produce habitual, focused giving. The explosion of new organizations and personal causes made easier by the Internet also competes for donation dollars. And will the Internet increase the challenges with fraud and accountability longtime issues for charities?

Some charities also worry that they will lose control of their message if they turn to an army of online individuals who personalize it.

But nonprofits have always had to search for—and adapt to—new fundraising methods. The Internet and young givers are a natural match.

17

Employers Are Monitoring Social Networking Sites

Lindsay Edelstein

Lindsay Edelstein is a writer and the promotions coordinator at the New York Post.

As the popularity of social networking sites such as MySpace and Facebook spreads, more and more employers—and potential employers—are using them as a tool to check up on the people who are working for, or may want to work for, them. Worries about unprofessional behavior some employees may exhibit in their off hours being tied to a company's name or reputation are driving more and more employers to search the Internet to see what their employees are up to when they aren't at their desks. Increasingly, career counselors and recruiters are advising college students and job seekers to forego having a MySpace or Facebook site, or severely limit the activities they post there.

When John Ambrose, 24, interviews for jobs as a legal associate, he doesn't cite his hobbies as "anything that doesn't involve reading boring law books" or describe himself as a "party mongerer"—and he certainly doesn't have Hot Chip's "Playboy" playing in the background.

Until recently, these were among the details Ambrose, a third-year law student at Pace University, freely shared with tens of millions of MySpace users, and anyone else who landed

"Caught in a Mouse Trap: Job Hunting? Be Careful What You Post on the Internet—Because Employers Are Watching" *New York Post*, March 19, 2007. Reproduced by permission. Available at http://www.nypost.com/seven/03192007/atwork/caught_in_a_mouse_trap_atwork_lindsay_edelstein.htm.

on his personal Web profile. He figured he'd just as soon not share them with potential employers, though—which is why he wisely privatized his profile before starting his job search.

Not all job applicants are so proactive—and more are learning to regret it. While most job seekers have been schooled on how to present themselves in a cover letter or an interview, many overlook another important way employers get an impression of them: by trolling the Web for anything they can find.

Which means if you've got a page on a social networking site featuring photos of you mauling the stripper at your buddy's bachelor party, or if you write a blog that details your binge-drinking and bed-hopping exploits, odds are they're going to find it.

"Like it or not, your Google results are your new resume."

"The average job hunter doesn't realize that their potential employer is going to run their name in quotes through a search engine and keep digging until they find the dirt," says Todd Malicoat, an Internet consultant and the founder of the techie blog stuntdubl.com.

"Like it or not, your Google results are your new resume."

Four out of five companies perform background checks on some or all employees, according to a survey by the recruiting and staffing firm Spherion. And these days that means hitting the Web, whether it's checking networking sites such as MySpace or Friendster or just Googling your name to see what comes up.

Adam Zoia, founder of the headhunting firm Glocap Industries, says he relies extensively on the Internet.

"When companies do background checks, it's becoming increasingly common for them to Google people. If that's linked to YouTube or any other site on you, the prospective employer is going to see that."

Digging Up Dirt

Ask recruiters and HR professionals, and you'll get any number of stories about job applicants who've gotten snared in the Web (even if they're reluctant to attach their names to the stories, for fear of opening the door to lawsuits).

Zoia relates a story of an asset-management company that was seriously considering an applicant for a job as a health-care analyst—until they ran an Internet search on him, and turned up an investment forum where he was freely sharing information about his current company's activities. Worried he'd dish about which stocks they were trading if he was hired, they decided to look elsewhere.

The human-resources manager for a major media conglomerate tells the story of a candidate whose page on My-Space got him into trouble when he applied for an entry-level sales job—not because of ill-advised Spring Break photos, but because it revealed his true ambition.

"It said his dream was to move to New York and become an actor, and that he was trying to get a full-time job to fund his trip—once he got settled here, he'd quit and pursue acting," she says. "Needless to say, the interviewer decided the guy wasn't right for the job."

Even after you're hired—sometimes well after it—online activities can become a problem.

The former creative director at a nonprofit near Union Square recalls deciding to do an Internet check on someone who was in the final stages of being hired for a job as a Web developer, after an exhaustive check of his resume and references.

"Using MySpace and to a lesser extent Facebook, we learned that he fancied himself quite the ladies' man. His suggestive screen name and provocative profile gave the whole office something to laugh about for hours." (They gave him the job anyway, but he didn't last long.)

Even after you're hired—sometimes well after it—online activities can become a problem. One of the stories that persuaded Ambrose to privatize his profile was from a friend who was reprimanded by a boss who saw his MySpace page, which made reference both to drug use and to the company he worked for, and listed the company's Web site.

"He felt that the guy shouldn't be listing his job alongside his other exploits—some of them being illegal," says Ambrose.

The head of HR for a large Manhattan firm recalls a previous job in which a site manager got far worse than a reprimand after administrators found his personal Web page on an erotic dating site, which featured photos of him in various nude poses. He was fired.

"It wasn't illegal, but the reason given was that as a manager he showed extremely poor judgment by making such a personal matter public, undermining his credibility and losing the confidence of the staff," says the HR exec.

In other cases it might be less clear exactly what the harm is. Almost everyone has tied one on at some point, so why should you be afraid to talk about it on your MySpace page?

The issue is less knowing that you passed out under the bar at Coyote Ugly than knowing that you're telling the world about it, says Zoia—adding that even if employers don't judge you the worse for it, they might be concerned about how it reflects on the company.

"Everyone, including the most successful people, did things in their youth—that's not the issue," he says. "An employer won't say, 'If I ever heard you got drunk, you won't get hired.' It's more that you did those things and you're advertising it."

Likewise, when an internship applicant's Facebook profile advertised his interest in "Smokin' blunts with the homies and bustin' caps in whitey," Brad Karsh, the president of the job-services firm JobBound, understood he was just trying to be funny—but "it raised doubts about his judgment and professionalism," he says.

As a result of the growth of cyber-sleuthing, college career counselors are increasingly warning students about the pitfalls of letting it all hang out on the Web.

False Security

Even when job hunters think ahead and take down private information from the Internet, they forget that a lot of online content is cached and remains accessible to others for a certain period of time after it's been deleted. "People may think that they've taken something down, but it may be seen by a person that digs a little bit," says Zoia.

Others might feel protected by the walls around a site such as Facebook, where profiles can be seen only by other members. But some employers seem to be finding ways around that. Tracy Mitrano, the director of Internet technology at Cornell University, says that when she recently spoke to a group of students about IT policy, one student told her she'd been asked by a corporate employer to look up a job applicant's Facebook profile.

"When I asked if any other students had been in similar situations, about five people raised their hands," she says.

As a result of the growth of cyber-sleuthing, college career counselors are increasingly warning students about the pitfalls of letting it all hang out on the Web.

"We've begun to talk about the MySpace and Facebook dangers," says Bob Casper, director of career services at SUNY Oswego.

"Today's students have grown up in a wired world," he notes. "They may not be aware of the visibility they'll encounter by posting blogs and personal Web sites."

Many are wising up, though. In a recent survey, CollegeGrad.com found that 47 percent of college-grad job seekers who use social networking sites had changed or were planning to change the content of their pages.

"We tell people point-blank, do not have a MySpace page or a Facebook page. Period. The end."

Playing It Safe

Given the potential downside, are you better off avoiding networking sites and other Web activity entirely?

It depends whom you ask.

"We tell people point-blank, do not have a MySpace page or a Facebook page. Period. The end," says Zoia, whose high-paying clients include investment banks, venture capital funds and consultant firms. "Given that the stakes are high with these jobs, the level of scrutiny is high."

Top Internet recruiter Shally Steckerl takes less of a hard line, arguing that if you avoid coming across as a knucklehead, such pages can actually be helpful.

"It's OK, maybe even cool, to want to share your passion for movies, martial arts and Xbox 360—it shows that you're a three-dimensional person," he says.

Malicoat hopes that, as online background checks become more prevalent, companies will lower their expectations of online purity.

"A good employer will start to understand that if a marketing executive wants to have a few pictures online where they're out partying with friends that it might just be OK," he says. "I think the exposure to more of employees' personal lives will force employers to have a little bit more tolerance for extracurricular activities—or end up with bum employees with no personality."

18

Mobile Social Networking Software Has Pros and Cons

Gloria Goodale

Gloria Goodale is a staff reporter for the Christian Science Monitor. *Based in Los Angeles, she writes on arts and culture.*

The next wave of the virtual community, begun with the cyber-social networks such as MySpace and Facebook, is Mobile Social Networking Software, or MoSoSo. This software combines the social networking of on-line communities with global positioning technology, giving cell phones increased functionality, and users—wherever they are—a whole new world at their fingertips. Proponents of this technology are excited about the possibilities of MoSoSo, such as allowing the added safety of cyberescort services on college campuses. Others, however, worry about the increased likelihood of criminals being able to locate potential victims, as well as the growing antisocial behavior of students continually focused on their cyberworlds.

Walk on a college campus these days and you'll see cell-phones everywhere, but only some being used for conversations. Baruch College sophomore Yelena Slatkina in New York City recently rustled up an emergency sub at work by typing a plea to her entire work group on her cellphone. University of South Florida sophomore Nate Fuller routinely uses his cellphone equipped with Global Positioning Software (GPS) to find recruits for his intramural football team and locate friends in Tampa, Fla. Texas 21-year-old Brittany Bohnet uses photos she and 20 of her networked buddies snap on their phones to locate one another, using visual landmarks they spot in the pictures they send.

These under-25s (the target market for early adoption of hot new gadgets) are using what many observers call the next big consumer technology shift: Mobile Social Networking Software, or MoSoSo. The sophisticated reach of cyber-social networks such as MySpace or Facebook, combined with the military precision of GPS, is putting enough power in these students' pockets to run a small country.

But while many young users are enthralled with the extraordinary conveniences of what amounts to a personal-life remote control, others who have been tracking technology for more than a few semesters say that as the benefits of the multipurpose mobile phone expand, so do its risks. Not only do they point to possible security issues with GPS running on a cellphone, but cultural observers worry about the growing preference of young users to stay plugged into a virtual network, often oblivious to the real world around them.

With a society that is increasingly amusing and distracting itself to death, what's at stake is nothing less than the collective conscience.

"These technologies are addictive," says author Michael Bugeja, bemoaning what he calls a growing self-absorption encouraged by social networking. "With a society that is increasingly amusing and distracting itself to death, what's at stake is nothing less than the collective conscience."

The Iowa State University media professor, who has written extensively about the cultural impact of new technologies, suggests that an increased focus on networking only with likeminded folks could diminish the ability to deal with the unfamiliar—a skill that is vital to democratic institutions.

Pros and Con Artists

Mobile GPS will open a Pandora's box of possibilities, say others. "I'd be very concerned about pedophiles or identity thieves hacking into a system and locating me, my wife, or daughter," says Henry Simpson, who coordinates new technology for the California State University at Monterey Bay (CSUMB). "It raises huge safety issues," he adds.

But new technologies have always brought new risks—such as identity theft. Philosophically, every technology has both positive and negative values, says Andrew Anker, vice president of development at Six Apart, a Web consulting firm. "In fact," he points out, "the most positive aspects are what also add the most negative."

Companies looking to do business on college campuses have paid particular attention to security concerns. Rave Wireless introduced a GPS/MoSoSo enabled phone for students this past year, emphasizing the security value of the GPS feature over its potential to deliver underage victims to predators. While the Rave phones enable students to find likeminded buddies (Bored? Love Indian food? Meet me under the clock!), it also offers a cyberescort service linked to campus police. If the student doesn't turn off a timer in the phone, indicating safe arrival at a destination, police are dispatched to a GPS location.

Campus residents give the service high marks. Kristen Halverson, a resident adviser at CSUMB, says her students are often alone on campus late at night. "The GPS escort is probably the best new thing for students I've seen," she says.

There is a certain irony in the concerns about safety using GPS, points out industry analyst, Bijan Sabet, a partner at the venture capital firm, Spark Capital. Mobile GPS was created in response to a federal mandate, because cellphones couldn't handle 911 emergency calls. But, safety concerns aside, the phone is clearly the hot new platform in the tech world—witness [Apple co-founder] Steve Jobs's announcement of the Apple iPhone. "It's not a matter of 'if' the mobile phone will prove important, it's just a matter of how fast," adds Mr. Sabet.

MoSoSo: The New Social Glue

The phone is the primary tool for planning and organizing lives today, says Rave CEO Roger Desai. He argues that rather than undermining a larger civic awareness, the combination of mobile social networks with GPS has the potential to reinvigorate moribund civic areas, such as old downtown business zones. His company has been working with cities such as Newark, N.J., to connect people with their local attractions and services. "This is their opportunity to take back the community," says Mr. Desai, who says people can now open their phones and find the local taco stand or dry cleaner, often businesses they never knew existed.

Other firms are rushing to explore the possibilities of Mo-SoSo. Helio was one of the first to take the plunge, betting on the importance of the tiny tool. "Most of our users don't even have landlines anymore," says Michael Grossi, [wireless carrier] Helio's vice president of business development. The company's first MoSoSo phone did not have GPS; the current version, dubbed the "Drift," combines MySpace with GPS. Mr. Grossi is quick to point out that the locator function is strictly "opt in," meaning users can turn it on and off at will. The company does not store location information. "It's part of our ethic not to collect customer data," says Grossi. "Our purpose is to encourage communication and connection without any fear that Big Brother is watching."

Students have clearly connected with the mobile social networking worlds offered by their phones. Walking the campus at California State University, Los Angeles (CSULA), Samantha Jones is a typical student. Focused on the phone she grips in front of her, she's been texting and cyberchatting with friends all day, barely breaking her stride to eat or attend classes. The photo-happy Ms. Bohnet says she only tolerates actual phone calls—which take her attention off her network of friends—from her parents because they aren't up to speed with MoSoSo.

> Students have clearly connected with the mobile social networking worlds offered by their phones.

Social, or Antisocial, Tools?

But concerns over the self-absorption potential of social networking are also somewhat ironic to Gilbert Gonzales, chief information officer for CSUMB. The campus sought out a contract with Rave Wireless, in part to help combat growing antisocial behavior created by the Internet on campus. "Students were stuck in their rooms using the Internet on their computers," says Mr. Gonzales. By allowing them to become mobile, he hopes to get students back out onto the campus to connect with other students.

While phones are clearly omnipresent on campuses, naysayers can take small comfort that there is the occasional holdout. Possibly one of the few college students on the planet not to own a cellphone, Carlos Rodriguez says he prefers interacting with others in person. "I like the subtlety of a human face—you can't get that on the phone, in a picture, or using GPS," says the CSULA electrical-engineering major. "I'd rather meet somebody and interact in person," he adds. "It's just a richer experience. No phone or any other technology can replace that."

Organizations to Contact

The editors have compiled the following list of organizations concerned with the issues debated in this book. The descriptions are derived from materials provided by the organizations. All have publications or information available for interested readers. The list was compiled on the date of publication of the present volume; the information provided here may change. Be aware that many organizations may take several weeks or longer to respond to inquiries, so allow as much time as possible.

American Library Association (ALA)
50 E. Huron, Chicago, IL   60611
(800) 545-2433
Web site: www.ala.org

ALA is the oldest and largest library association in the world, with more than sixty-five thousand members. Its mission is to promote the highest quality library and information services and public access to information. ALA offers professional services and publications to members and nonmembers, including online news stories.

Center for Democracy and Technology (CDT)
1634 Eye St. NW, Suite 1100, Washington, DC   20006
(202) 637-9800 • fax: (202) 637-0968
e-mail: info@cdt.org
Web site: www.cdt.org

CDT's mission is to develop public policy solutions that advance constitutional civil liberties and democratic values in new computer and communications media. Pursuing its mission through policy research, public education, and coalition building, the center works to increase citizens' privacy and the public's control over the use of personal information held by government and other institutions. Its publications include issue briefs, policy papers, and *CDT Policy Posts*, an online, occasional publication that covers issues regarding the civil liberties of those using the information highway.

Center for Digital Media Freedom (CDMF)

The Progress & Freedom Foundation, Washington, DC   20005
(202) 289-8928 • fax: (202) 289-6079
e-mail: mail@pff.org
Web site: www.pff.org

Maintained by the Progress & Freedom Foundation, the CDMF promotes liberal public policy regarding all forms of communications, as well the freedom of speech and expression. Its goal is maximizing media freedom both in a structural (business) sense and a social (speech-related) sense.

Electronic Frontier Foundation (EFF)

454 Shotwell St., San Francisco, CA   94110-1914
(415) 436 9333 • fax: (415) 436 9993
e-mail: eff@eff.org
Web site: www.eff.org

EFF is an organization of students and other individuals that aims to promote a better understanding of telecommunications issues. It fosters awareness of civil liberties issues arising from advancements in computer-based communications media and supports litigation to preserve, protect, and extend First Amendment rights in computing and telecommunications technologies. EFF's publications include *Building the Open Road, Crime and Puzzlement*, the quarterly newsletter *Networks & Policy*, the biweekly electronic newsletter *EFFector Online*, and online bulletins and publications, including *First Amendment in Cyberspace*.

Internet Society (ISOC)

1775 Wiehle Ave., Suite 102, Reston, VA   20190-5108
(703) 326-9880 • fax: (703) 326-9881
e-mail: isoc@isoc.org
Web site: www.isoc.org

A group of technologists, developers, educators, researchers, government representatives, and businesspeople, ISOC supports the development and dissemination of standards for the Internet and works to ensure global cooperation and coordination for the Internet and related Internet-working technologies and applications. It publishes the bimonthly magazine *On the Internet*.

OnGuard Online

Federal Trade Commission (FTC), Washington, D.C.   20580
e-mail: onlineonguard@ftc.gov
Web site: http://onguardonline.gov

Maintained by the FTC, OnGuardOnline.gov provides practical tips from the federal government and the technology industry to help Internet users combat Internet fraud, secure their computers, and protect their personal information.

Save Your Space

c/o the Friends of MySpace, Yorba Linda, CA   92886
(888) 277-5099 • fax: (253) 681-0754
Web site: www.saveyourspace.org

The Save Your Space petition was created by the Friends of MySpace, a social networking advocacy organization based in Orange County, California, in response to bill HR 5319 submitted by U.S. Representative Michael Fitzpatrick in mid-2006. The petition benefits all users and operators of social networking, blogging, and chat room sites.

WiredSafety

Web site: www.wiredsafety.org

Run entirely by volunteers and founded in 1995, WiredSafety is the largest online safety, education, and help group in the world. It is a cyber Neighborhood Watch and operates worldwide in cyberspace through its more than nine thousand volunteers. The Web site offers Internet users a place to report Internet crimes, including cyberstalking, harassment, and child pornography.

Bibliography

Books

W.D. Edmiston

Why Parents Should Fear MySpace. Longwood, FL: Xulon, 2007.

Allison Fine

Momentum: Igniting Social Change in the Connected Age. San Francisco: Jossey-Bass, 2006.

Gerard Goggin

Cell Phone Culture: Mobile Technology in Everyday Life. New York: Routledge, 2006.

Jay Liebowitz

Social Networking: The Essence of Innovation. Lanham, MD: Rowman & Littlefield, 2007.

Sydney Eve Matrix

Cyberpop: Digital lifestyles and Commodity Culture. New York: Routledge, 2006.

Mark Nunes

Cyberspaces of Everyday Life. Minneapolis: University of Minnesota Press, 2006.

Christian and Amy Piatt

MySpace to Sacred Space: God for a New Generation. Duluth, GA: Chalice, 2007.

Howard Rheingold

Smart Mobs: The Next Social Revolution. New York: Basic Books, 2003.

Max Taylor and Ethel Quayle

Child Pornography: An Internet Crime. New York: Brunner-Routledge, 2003.

Periodicals

Megan Bakker — "The Dangerous Trend of Posting Personal Information on MySpace," *Collegian*, April 19, 2006.

Mark Boslet — "Two Different Neighborhoods in Cyberspace," *San Jose Mercury News*, August 5, 2007.

Thomas Claburn — "Second Life Loses Gamblers but Finds God," *InformationWeek*, July 30, 2007.

Laura Deeley — "I'm Single, I'm Sexy, and I'm Only 13," *Times* (London), July 28, 2007.

Chris DeWolf — "The MySpace Generation," *Forbes*, May 7, 2007.

Odvard Egil Dyrli — "Online Social Networking: Sites Such as MySpace, Facebook and Xanga are Transforming Teen Cultures," *District Administration*, March 1, 2006.

Geoffrey H. Fletcher — "Power Up, Don't Power Down: Barring Students from Using Cell Phones, MySpace, and Other Communication Technologies Once They Enter the Classroom Is the Wrong Approach," *Technical Horizons in Education*, September 1, 2006.

Maryann James — "Jane Is Listed as Single; All of Facebook Knows It," *Baltimore Sun*, August 4, 2007.

Janet Kornblum	"Rudeness, Threats Make the Web a Cruel World," *USA Today*, July 30, 2007.
Steven Levy	"Social Networking and Class Warfare," *Newsweek International*, August 13, 2007.
Nikki Schwab and Sean Dustman	"The World of Military Blogging," *Washington Post*, May 3, 2007.
Alan Sipress and Sam Diaz	"A Casualty of War: MySpace," *Washington Post*, May 15, 2007.
Michelle Slatalla	"Online Worlds Give Kids a Chance to Run Their Own Show," *New York Times*, May 6, 2007.
Brad Stone	"On Facebook, a Rising Concern Over Predators," *Boston Globe*, July 30, 2007.
Mark Sullivan	"A MySpace Law? Let's Get Real About Online Communities," *PC World*, July 25, 2007.

Index